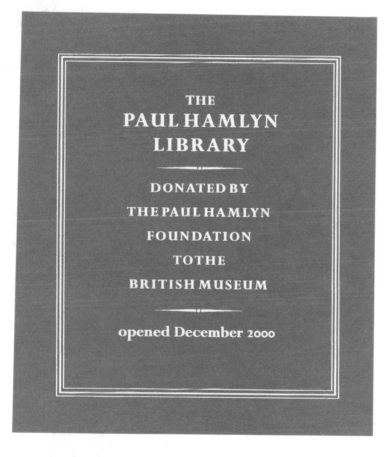

Lorenzo The Magnificent

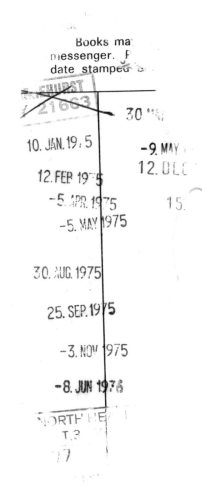

LORENZO
THE MAGNIFICENT

Maurice Rowdon

WEIDENFELD AND NICOLSON
LONDON

Designed by Trevor Vincent for
George Weidenfeld and Nicolson Limited
11 St. John's Hill
London sw 11
Picture research by Liz Drury of Harriet Bridgeman Ltd,
and Michelle Mason
Maps drawn by Design Practitioners Ltd

Filmset by Keyspools Ltd,
Golborne, Lancs.
Printed in England by
Tinling (1973) Ltd.

ISBN 0 297 76576 0

Contents

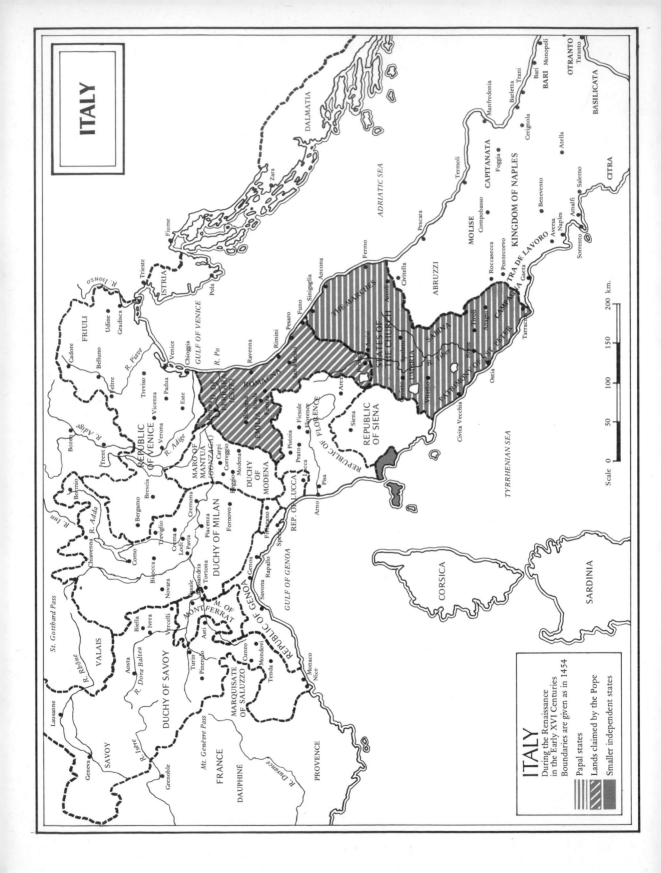

ITALY

During the Renaissance
in the Early XVI Centuries
Boundaries are given as in 1454

Papal states

Lands claimed by the Pope

Smaller independent states

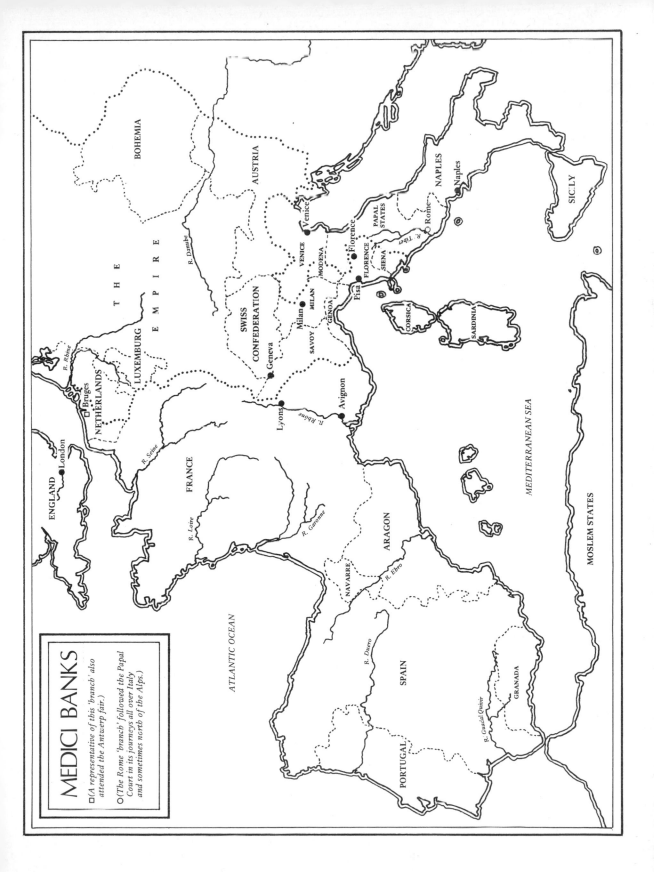

MEDICI BANKS

□ (A representative of this 'branch' also
attended the Antwerp fair.)

○ (The Rome 'branch' followed the Papal
Court in its journeys all over Italy
and sometimes north of the Alps.)

BOHEMIA

AUSTRIA

NAPLES

Naples

SIC.LY

THE

EMPIRE

R. Danube

VENICE
Venice

PAPAL
STATES

Rome

FLORENCE
Florence
MODENA
FLORENCE
SIENA

SWISS
CONFEDERATION

MILAN
Milan

Pisa

CORSICA

SARDINIA

LUXEMBURG

GENOA

SAVOY

Geneva

R. Rhine

Bruges

NETHERLANDS

London

ENGLAND

R. Rhône

Lyons

Avignon

MEDITERRANEAN SEA

R. Seine

FRANCE

MOSLEM STATES

R. Loire

R. Garonne

NAVARRE

ARAGON

R. Ebro

ATLANTIC OCEAN

R. Duero

SPAIN

PORTUGAL

GRANADA

R. GuadalQuivir

INTRODUCTION

Lorenzo de' Medici was twenty one when he took over the government of Florence in December 1469. He was none too anxious to inherit from his father a 'throne' which was no throne at all, nor even an official position. The Florentines were an ungrateful lot, and it seemed much easier to remain a rich, popular and astonishingly gifted young man, known to every prince in Europe as the inheritor of the Medici millions and the most princely patron of thought and art in Christendom. It was a tough decision, and one he had to make within a day of his father Piero's death. He knew too that most likely he himself would one day die of the same hereditary disease, gout, and that hard work and worry would make an early death probable. And he did die, worn out and crippled, at the age of forty three.

He preferred the family's country villas at Careggi, Fiesole, Cafaggiolo, Castello and many other places to the newly-built one in town. He enjoyed riding and hawking in the Pisan hills. He preferred peasants to politicians, and would spend hours talking to them and going round the various family farms. Above all, he loved to sit and write – songs and ballads, sonnets and perhaps the first drama, in our sense, ever written. His brilliant friend Pico della Mirandola thought him the equal of Dante and Petrarch: that might well have been true had he ever been allowed the necessary solitude. Certainly, without him the Italian language might have fallen into a long decay, swamped by an artificial Latin which every snob aspired to write without always writing it well. He could write both consummately. He was versatile – the most versatile of all the artists and thinkers, scholars and musicians, who sat round his dinner-table informally throughout his life. Yet he succeeded in escaping dilletantism.

His education, mainly under Gentile Becchi, was thorough without unnecessary pain and discipline. Italians were then, as now, most tolerant and sympathetic towards young people, and never pressed them too hard, or excluded them from adult company and adult pleasures. The result was remarkably mature children: Lorenzo was already an able diplomat at the age of sixteen, and a shrewd party-chief. He was the soul of courtesy. What the Italians call *simpatia* poured out of him, touched with authority and sometimes harshness. He could even joust, though without much enthusiasm: like most Florentines he was no fighter, and did not deliberately court danger. He could be vulgarly cutting when he thought it right, but was unpretentious and natural in his behaviour, which put him all right with the common people, an important asset if one had to govern the virtually ungovernable, as he did. Even his horse Morello stamped and neighed with pleasure when he came near the stables, and if sick refused his oats until his master served him.

Lorenzo was no beauty, despite Benozzo Gozzoli's portrait of him when he was ten in the *Magi* frescoes at the Medici town-house. He had a large nose, rather flattened at the bridge and curling to a bulbous end,

OPPOSITE A terracotta bust of Lorenzo by Verrocchio or his school. Verrocchio (1435–88) was among Lorenzo's favourite artists.

OVERLEAF Villa Medici at Fiesole.

The courtyard of the Palazzo Medici in Florence. At the wedding feast for Lorenzo de' Medici and Clarice Orsini (1469) the older male guests sat under these arches.

RIGHT A detail from *The Journey of the Magi* by Benozzo Gozzoli in the chapel of the Medici palace in Florence. The fresco was commissioned in 1459 by Piero de' Medici, Lorenzo's father, who asked Benozzo to paint it in the 'antique' style of Fra' Angelico and Gentile da Fabriano. It shows the Medici country villa at Cafaggiolo.

A detail from Domenico Ghirlandaio's *Apparition of the Angel to Zacharias in the Temple*, a fresco in the church of S. Maria Novella, Florence. The portraits here are of the neo-Platonists in Lorenzo's circle: Marsilio Ficino, Agnolo Poliziano, Cristoforo Landino and Lorenzo's teacher from Urbino (later Bishop of Areggo) Gentile Becchi.

OPPOSITE A detail from *The Battle of San Romano* by Paolo Uccello (1397–1475) showing the *condottiere* Niccolo da Tolentino leading the Florentine troops to victory against their traditional enemies the Sienese on 1 June 1432. The Sienese were raiding Florentine territory, as they often did in the fifteenth century.

yet no sense of smell. His chin was powerful to the point of suggesting brutality, though a less vindictive or repressive ruler (at least until the attempt on his life in Florence's cathedral) could hardly be imagined. It was the chin of a determined and infinitely patient man. His voice was rather irritating, nasal and grating, and could easily be heard above those of his servants when the household choir was performing his songs. His personality was all the more fascinating for these apparent drawbacks. He had what is perhaps the most important asset in politics, the ability to enter another man's world the moment he clapped eyes on him. It was once said of him that with the poet he was a poet, with the ambassador a man of state and with the blackguard a blackguard-and-a-half. That was not a very Italian characteristic, which meant that he was always one step ahead of the people round him. He could delve sympathetically into the other man's heart, reading there the needs and hopes and calculations. Men felt understood in his presence. And he was trusted, for the simple reason that he was trustworthy: even his enemies granted him that. There were mistakes in his government, and as many shady deals as under his grandfather Cosimo, but no treachery.

Above all, he was quick to encourage. Passing through Ghirlandaio's studio one day, he happened to see a faun's mask carved in marble. He stopped and pointed out to the boy-apprentice that such an old faun would have a few teeth missing. That boy was Michelangelo. He at once struck out a front tooth with his chisel. Later Lorenzo persuaded the boy's father to let him live in his household, which was really a Court without livery. The boy sat next to him at table, and on free afternoons

Lorenzo took him to see his latest acquisitions – a brooch, a piece of ancient statuary just arrived from Rome, a marble cup from the third century AD set on a new silver base. Michelangelo was clothed at his expense. For eighteen years, the family accepted him as an adopted son. As a bribe, Lorenzo offered the boy's father, a rather poor yeoman called Buonarotti, any job he liked to name. The man chose a low position in the customs office. 'You'll never get rich like that', Lorenzo told him. A Medici would have asked for a chancellorship, or at least a post in the tax-assessor's office (failing a round sum of money).

Of course, the world was at Lorenzo's feet long before his father died. The family name resounded everywhere in Europe, and spelled 'gold'. There was hardly a head of state who had not had a fat loan from one of the Medici banks, or dreamed of one. England's Edward IV had fought his wars and won them on Medici money. No French envoy passed through Florence without Medici gifts being loaded on him to sweeten his journey to or from Rome, in the interests of that Paris-Florence *entente* which was so much the secret of Florentine diplomacy over the years. Lorenzo grew up in this atmosphere of largesse and fame. He was the first 'prince' of the Medici family, which had hitherto ruled as simple business men, keeping out of the public eye and particularly out of the great aristocratic festivities. He loved pretty women, and was unaccustomed to being refused: not that this was a departure from family tradition (both his grandfather Cosimo and his father Piero had had bastard children), only now it was allowed a public and chivalrous tone. He enjoyed roaming Florence or the outlying villages for the unexpected affair, with Pulci the writer or Botticelli the painter. The chamberlain of his household once wrote to him that Pulci seemed to be 'the little spirit in his balls', referring ambiguously to the six balls of the Medici coat-of-arms.

Florence's top political men called at the family house in Via Larga (by now a political headquarters for the Medici party) during his father Piero's last hours. They came again and again. He gave a polite 'no' to their request that he take over. They pointed out that there must be no gap in the city's government. He pointed out that he wanted a quiet life and was too young for the responsibility.

But the day after his father's death he accepted. The gap was all too evident. He realised that to go on being a Medici, even to go on being privately influential, he must run the state as his father and his grandfather had done. The family's banking business was virtually a political network throughout Italy and in many of the capitals north of the Alps. One could not run that sort of business without taking a lead in Florence's government. One could not have the necessary relations with foreign princes unless one were something akin to a prince at home. Lorenzo knew that within a year of starting a private life his influence would have ceased and another rich family would have gained control of the city,

OPPOSITE A detail from *A Hunt*, oil on panel by Paolo Uccello, perhaps from a chest commissioned by Federigo da Montefeltro, the Duke of Urbino. It is thought to represent the young Lorenzo de' Medici hunting in the woods around Pisa, where he owned much land.

OVERLEAF A detail from Benozzo Gozzoli's fresco *The Journey of the Magi*, showing Lorenzo mounted on a horse at the age of ten in a somewhat idealised portrait.

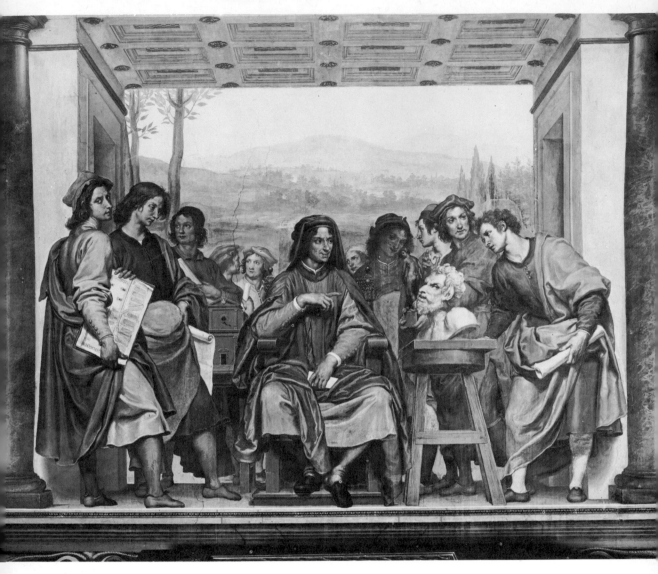

A scene from a fresco in the Pitti palace by Ottavio Vannini. Lorenzo, in the centre, is admiring a bust of a faun by Michelangelo, who as a young man was one of Lorenzo's circle of Florentine artists.

which meant the city's system of taxation. It would be a matter of months for that family to manipulate the taxes against the Medici interest, and perhaps reduce the family fortune to a particle of what it was at this moment. Even to go on enjoying the simple things of his youth, he must govern. A fallen Medici would soon be a banished Medici, since even when weak the family would be feared as a possible source of revolution.

It had not been to pay Lorenzo's grandfather an empty posthumous compliment that the ruling men of Florence had given him the title 'Pater Patriae', in the style of the Roman empire. It was simply that he had made himself, by seeing his own interests as those of the state, no less than the 'father of the fatherland'. Cosimo's private fortune had gone into entertaining foreign princes and envoys, just as the public purse had been opened to prop up his business when it looked like tottering. That was why Florence's greatest families were so anxious to get Lorenzo onto the 'throne' as soon as possible, because up to a certain point (that point being where they felt effective and dangerous rivals) his interests were theirs.

It was no small thing to govern Florence. It was the most important centre of cloth-production for southern Europe. Since the thirteenth century it had become increasingly rich, and exclusively commercial. It was the first city to form a capitalist society in which money-interests and not landed or Church or monarchical ones governed. The weavers had always been wage-earners in the service of merchants. These merchants had travelled and procured the export trade. By the first half of the thirteenth century Florentine merchants were sending cloth as far as the Orient, and importing their wool from England, their silk from Lombardy. It naturally gave them a hold on city-life, since they quickly became the key to city-fortunes. During the thirteenth century the 'money-changers' or bankers of Florence and Siena were active in every part of Europe. They were generally known as 'Lombards' (the pawn-brokers of the Middle Ages), and Lombard Street in London's City owes its name to them. Long before the Medici family came on the scene, Sienese bankers like Musciatto de' Francesi and Guidi were acting as agents to the pope, and as collectors, treasurers and financial advisers to other princes. The Sienese company of Bonsignori went bankrupt in 1298 after being the chief banking group in Christendom. It was this bankruptcy that brought Florence to the centre of financial affairs in Europe. The Florentine gold florin, minted from 1252 onwards, became the most stable and universally respected currency in Europe, a gold standard of the time.

The money-men and the merchants, in mixing with princes and popes, became a new political power that the landed nobility had to reckon with. They married into the nobility quite often, just as the nobility entered finance and trade. Florence, in this too, was the most forward in development, so much so that the landed nobility was quickly reduced to second place by clever political manipulation. The nobles had to 'move into' town. If they wanted political influence, they had to give up being noble and join one of the trade guilds. All the big merchant families of Florence were enrolled in one of the seven major trade guilds or *arti*. The so-called 'lesser' guilds or *arti minori* covered the less important consumer trades, and much of Florence's history at that time was the story of their struggle with the greater guilds for political supremacy.

Florence was more than a city. Even in the eleventh century it had included the country district to the north and east of its walls called the Mugello, as well as the Chianti land to the south, half-way to Siena. Between the eleventh and fourteenth centuries it had spread across another, vaster country district called the Casentino to the east and south, taking in the city of Arezzo as well as Pistoia to the north-west and

Volterra to the south-west. By the beginning of the fifteenth century, the Florentine state stretched along the Chiana valley in the south to within ten miles of Lake Trasimene, which made a number of popes sleep less soundly at night. Under the Medici, it spread to both the Mediterranean and – through its satellite states – the Adriatic coast. Needless to say, the city's prosperity, its diplomatic prestige in the Courts of Europe (where its money sweetened many bad tempers in the course of time), together with its provocative taste for the republican way of life, made some bitter and dangerous enemies. In the period of its greatest power under the Medici, the republic was rarely free of menace.

But the menace was greatest from inside the city. Florence's history, before it became a ducal backwater some years after Lorenzo's death, was politically the most violent in Europe. Little blood was shed, as it all took the form of arguing. The constitution changed even more times than the government. Committees of reform (the famous *Balìe*) were in session almost constantly during the period of the Medicean republic. There were assassinations, revolutions, *coups d'état*. There was a constant jockeying for position among the big families, constant bribery and intimidation, and manipulation of votes or taxes by the families in power, to secure or prevent a monopoly. Most historians seem to have thought this simply a matter of Florentine character. But the reason for it lay less in Florentine vitality than in the social restlessness caused by financial operations which more and more dominated the city's life and determined the amount of work and money available, not to say the degree of political influence abroad.

Florence's highly modern condition has since spread to the rest of the world, and social restlessness has become virtually an accepted condition of life, as indeed it was in fifteenth-century Florence. We are therefore perhaps in a good position to understand the predicament of rulers and ruled alike in the city. There were sudden and unexplained periods of unemployment, even famine. There were equally sudden and equally unexplained periods of full employment and prosperity. All the Medici leaders of the republic during the fifteenth century – Giovanni di Averardo (1360–1429), Cosimo (1389–1464), Piero (1416–1469) and Lorenzo – experienced these crises: and once they had got into politics, under Cosimo, they tried to deal with them by new fiscal programmes and budgets, much as a government does today. Some of these measures, such as Lorenzo's manipulation of the currency towards the end of his life, were bitterly unpopular.

Even the restless imagination of the Florentine that drew so many thinkers and artists such as Pico della Mirandola and Perugino within its walls, and produced a more astonishing testimony of 'rebirth' than anywhere else in Christendom, was partly accountable to the turbulence of the society. The search for ancient manuscripts that went on under Cosimo, Piero and Lorenzo was due not entirely or even mostly to

GIOVANNI DI BICCI DE MEDICI

A portrait of Giovanni di Averardo Bicci de' Medici (1360–1429), founder of the Medici dynasty, by Angelo Bronzino who lived a century later and probably followed an earlier portrait by Masaccio, now lost.

BELOW The genealogical tree of the Medici family.

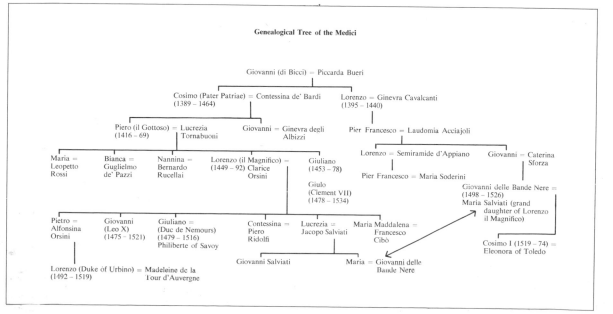

Genealogical Tree of the Medici

Giovanni (di Bicci) = Piccarda Bueri

Cosimo (Pater Patriae) = Contessina de' Bardi (1389 – 1464)   Lorenzo = Ginevra Cavalcanti (1395 – 1440)

Piero (il Gottoso) = Lucrezia Tornabuoni (1416 – 69)   Giovanni = Ginevra degli Albizzi   Pier Francesco = Laudomia Acciajoli

Maria = Leopetto Rossi   Bianca = Guglielmo de' Pazzi   Nannina = Bernardo Rucellai   Lorenzo (il Magnifico) = Clarice Orsini (1449 – 92)   Giuliano (1453 – 78)   Lorenzo = Semiramide d'Appiano   Giovanni = Caterina Sforza

Giulo (Clement VII) (1478 – 1534)   Pier Francesco = Maria Soderini

Giovanni delle Bande Nere = (1498 – 1526) Maria Salviati (grand daughter of Lorenzo il Magnifico)

Pietro = Alfonsina Orsini   Giovanni (Leo X) (1475 – 1521)   Giuliano = (Duc de Nemours) (1479 – 1516) Philiberte of Savoy   Contessina = Piero Ridolfi   Lucrezia = Jacopo Salviati   Maria Maddalena = Francesco Cibò

Cosimo I (1519 – 74) = Eleonora of Toledo

Lorenzo (Duke of Urbino) = Madeleine de la (1492 – 1519)   Tour d'Auvergne   Giovanni Salviati   Maria = Giovanni delle Bande Nere

curiosity. It was rather like the long discussions about immortality that Lorenzo enjoyed so much with his friends Poliziano and Ficino, and like his grandfather's study of Plato's works: a desperate search for stability.

Florence was a great financial centre at a time when the dangers of an interest-rate and promissory notes had not been fully experienced or understood. The restlessness was total. The promissory notes subsidised new building projects, even new states, just as they subsidised year-long searches for ancient manuscripts in every part of Asia and Europe. It is difficult for us today to realise what extraordinary new hope arose from the fact that one could plan a dazzling future for oneself, as a pope or prince or business man, without taking account of the fact that one had no money. Borrowing released what we call the Renaissance far more than any other factor. Florence searched for artists and scholars and musicians, it hired out its human treasures to other princes and ordered designs from the finest architects – all, so to speak, in one breath. There seemed nothing on earth that Florence could not interest herself in. The discussions at the little 'Platonic academy' round Lorenzo took in everything from the Cabbala to village superstitions in the Abruzzi. The city was giddy with thought. It was the giddiness of an immense banking operation which saw everything, from Flemish pictures to a foreign war, as an exciting investment.

Thus the Medici were nothing like the princes they rubbed shoulders with and increasingly influenced. They were more like modern financiers who have a hidden finger in politics and can exercise a devastating pressure when they really have to. On the other hand, everyone knew that a Medici was behind the scenes, and addressed his petitions to him. In this the great city was deliberately hypocritical. It asked for a man to govern who had more money than anyone else, but to govern in such a way that it would feel as if no one was governing at all. The Florentine hated restraints. He did not like princes, except as ten-day visitors (if they were nice people). He did not like chaos either. In fact, knowing what an unruly person he himself was, he took as many steps to prevent chaos as he did to secure freedom: hence the changes of constitution and the well-nigh obsessive conditions and restraints that fettered every atom of power. Chaos and freedom made odd bedfellows, and the result was bursts of strong government alternating with periods of utter confusion.

Lorenzo, being conscientious and highly sensitive, suffered the ups and downs of the state he controlled, and the finances he manipulated. It wrecked his nervous system. He foresaw that this would be so. He knew that the artistic and humanistic side of the times, what we now call the Renaissance, was financed by the money side and yet at variance with it. The two were bound together. Frescoes on chapel walls, discussion groups in the woods at Calmaldoli, carnival processions designed with taste, evenings of music, not to mention salaries and pensions for writers and painters and sculptors and musicians, all had to be paid for. It was natural that the city should stretch itself beyond its powers, rather as Lorenzo stretched himself. He may even have foreseen that he would be not simply the climax of Medici rule but its death, as far as a great and independent state was concerned. He certainly saw that the neo-classical movement could easily become artificial, which was why he cultivated his friendship with Pulci, the tavern-poet. He even seemed to have an inkling that since money was at the bottom of everything artistic in the city – every painter's studio and monastery-library and university lecture-room – then these things too were at the mercy of money, which was up one day and down the next.

Like his father Piero, he never held an official position in the city. His grandfather Cosimo had been three times something akin to chief justice (*Gonfaloniere della Giustizia*), but for a total period of only six months. Lorenzo was never old enough for that office, for which a man qualified only at forty-five. He remained a private citizen, and to all intents and purposes a humble one, who stepped aside in the street when an older man passed and was careful to make it clear in all his actions that he was Florence's servant rather than its tyrant.

Yet he was the hub of government. No important decision was taken without his advice. This does not mean that he was a kind of beneficent chancellor of the exchequer. The power of money was absolute. With his finger on the tax laws, he could make or unmake a man, though he always had to consider that too many rich men in opposition might over-turn his empire. Money enabled him to secure a degree of personal control not unlike a dictatorship. Many people did think him a tyrant, particularly in his later years, but they were his enemies, most of whom wanted to supplant his 'tyranny' with theirs.

It was not simply that the Medici knew how to make money. In a very real sense, they brought it into being. They did not invent banks or percentages: the Venetians had devised the *per cento* calculation three centuries before, during the Crusades, and banking had been practised for at least two centuries. 'Bank' simply referred to the table or *banco* at which the man with the money sat, lending or storing it. The genius of the Medici was to see that money, above all the promise of money and the charging of interest, could be made the central operation of life on which all other things, from relations with foreign states to popularity at home, could be made to depend. Perhaps more than any other group of men, they spelled the ruin of the Middle Ages, when little profit had been made and usury had been forbidden as a disaster to society, virtually a guarantee of constant friction. Medieval society had produced the amount of food it needed and not the amount it could have. Its system of self-reliant domains and walled towns had come into being, as a desperate attempt at survival against exorbitant imperial taxes (which hit the small-holder) and not least the roaming brigands. Roman roads fell into disuse. Ports declined. The Roman empire was a bad memory.

The end of the medieval period came when Europe was no longer afraid. It was rich and secure enough to face its own roots in the ancient world. It wanted to ply the seas again. Somehow or other, people seemed to want, in what sometimes looked like pleasant excitement and at others a mad frenzy, to reshape life. Here lay the 'rebirth' or the Renaissance, with the ancient world as the model. And money was the vehicle of these new extravagant hopes. The banker's note seemed the very token of dreams which sped beyond frontiers, seas, races, climates, in an increasingly global manifestation which even today has hardly finished its course. The little promissory note contained it all, gave possibility to all. It created new cities, new states, a new Church, new aristocracies, a new morality.

The Church formally and consciously dismantled the Middle Ages by admitting, indeed establishing, the respectability of 'taking money beyond the capital lent'. This does not mean that during the Middle Ages no profit had been made by merchants, or that no interest had been charged on loans. A constant argument had gone on between the merchants and the theologians as to what constituted honest business practice. Medieval business was controlled much more strictly and conscientiously than business ever has been since. The result was that interest had to be given another name. It hid under the so-called bills of exchange between one merchant and another: the sum returned was higher than the sum lent, and the difference could be classified as a gift or just compensation for the risk taken. It could also masquerade as a pure money exchange between two currencies. The rule that *usura solum in mutuo cadit*, or that usury applied only to a loan, meant that all one had to do was disguise the loan as something else.

Yet the idea of usury still aroused disapproval in the time of the Medici, and they themselves would have been shocked to hear themselves described as usurers. But the fact was that loaning operations, drawing an interest, were the main activity of the Medici company, far more important than its trading or manufacturing interests. These operations not only spread in the Christian world but became the basis of state politics, so much that it was soon accepted for the state to live on a debt. Florence was among the first states to create a balance of payments in deficit. That was the difference with the Middle Ages. It was a question of degree, and the strict distinction of nineteenth-century historians between 'the Middle Ages' and 'the Renaissance' has led to a false picture of what was in fact a slow and gradual development from earliest Christian times. The Medici were important not so much because they were great bankers – there had been greater bankers before them, like the Bardi and the Peruzzi companies – but because they understood and exploited the new role of money at a crucial time.

Once the new principle was accepted, a ruler could enter the most grandiose schemes on the basis of a promissory note, the loan to be repaid

A fourteenth-century miniature showing bankers counting money (above) and recording transactions (below). It was the development of accounting skills which permitted the early rise of international finance in Italy and the eventual founding of the Medici bank by Lorenzo's great-grandfather Giovanni di Bicci de' Medici.

when he had won his war or secured his throne or bribed his way into a useful dynastic connection. It was little wonder that society became turbulent, and that mounting prosperity was accompanied everywhere by mounting violence. The Medici understood the new connection between financial calculation and power, but they were as baffled as anyone by the violence. They produced the most modern state in Christendom out of this understanding, a state to which almost everyone turned for advice not only on politics but on thought and art and scholarship. This explains perhaps why Lorenzo's writings have such a modern tone, and have survived the mountains of other work produced at that time: the future world came into being in Florence's image. It was also what made Lorenzo one of the most remarkable rulers who has ever lived. He seemed always to be thinking several epochs ahead of other people.

Yet of all the Medici reigns, his was the most uncertain, while being apparently the most spectacular and successful. Lorenzo was baffled by the financial machinery at his disposal no less than his father Piero had been. It did not behave according to safe laws. It was influenced by invisible and distant factors over which they had no control. Though the Medici bank lasted for about a hundred years, it simply followed a period of expansion in the first half of its life, under Averardo and Cosimo, and then a period of gradual decline in its second half. There was no steady consolidation. Lorenzo was the witness of its spectacular decline, long before all its assets were liquidated by the state of Florence after his death. Several factors were responsible for this, and ones over which he had no control: trade to and from the Levant was no longer stable, because of the threat from the Turks; above all, the powers north of the Alps grew strong enough in his lifetime to disregard the sums they owed to the Medici bank. Wealth was seen to be a dangerous basis for political power after all. However much influence Lorenzo had with foreign princes, it could not compensate for the fact that he was the chief victim of the uncertain money market. However popular he was, however successful in his diplomatic *coups* during the years of his neutrality in the last decade of his life, no guarantee could be found against a market which seemed to follow its own course and threaten to reduce his position in a moment to that of another prince's satellite. There was the fact too that he was no financier, or even business man.

Dante had seen Florence as a sick man continually turning over in bed to avoid pain, and never finding the right position. The Medici were simply the human result of a long period of collective searching, and of one failed constitution after another. Admittedly the constitutional turmoil went on only on the surface. The factions which raced through the town on horseback, swords waving, to worry other factions, were rather harmless 'humours', and were called that. Florence before the time of the Medici was a sweet, intimate and above all gay town, looking rather different from today. Those neo-classical fronts were missing. The vast cupola and tower belonging to the cathedral did not at that time dominate the plain with their checkerwork. Nor were those overpowering 'rustic' walls to be seen, one stone neatly placed on another in what the Renaissance supposed to be the style of the Etruscans, as in the Medici, Strozzi and Pitti palaces. The river was not yet thrown open to the gaze. But the Ponte Vecchio, with its houses crammed together, was there. And the Santa Croce square, where the annual jousts took place, and the horseraces or *Palio*, looked much the same even as it does today. We have an excellent picture of medieval Florence if we keep to the narrow, paved side-lanes which curl round on each other and emerge in tiny, characteristically Florentine corners that are not exactly squares but the result of intensive rebuilding from several directions at once.

Prosperity was always Florence's objective. It accounted for the gaiety, the relative gaiety, just as in Italy today Tuscany's more industrial towns, such as Poggibonsi, Empoli or Montevarchi, seem happier and more bustling places than the purely rural ones, despite their eyesores. This belongs to the distinctive Tuscan temper: the Tuscan by tradition is Italy's man of business and a hard worker, though the business was always (and largely still is) rural business. Intelligence, the power of shrewd analysis, was the mark of his mind. Yet it was combined with a gift for intimate life, and a certain delicacy of taste, that sweetened the tendency to rather ruthless calculation. The result of this sweetness was perhaps the loveliest breed of women in Christendom, the most perfectly-spoken Italian, which became over the centuries the national speech, and a traditional distaste for brutality.

Florence was clearly not the place for princely Courts or a landed nobility or a military governor, though at different times in its history it experienced all of these. The intelligence went with a certain spirit of freedom that could be detected in the talk, even the walk, and the songs, and the wittily provocative way of the women. Clarice Orsini, Lorenzo the Magnificent's Roman wife, found this distressing and, while remaining a dutiful mother and estate-manager, she never got used to it. It was the opposite of anything she had known in the sleepily southern, rather staid palaces of Rome that one might describe as inhibited when compared with those of Florence.

Yet Florence was not in an outstandingly advantageous natural position. Her swift river did run to the Pisan coast, and she had protective mountains to the north, fertile hills to the south as far as Siena, but she lay in a saucer which drew mists, and prolonged the *scirocco*. The heat was unbearable when it came, and the cold from the Apennines in the winter biting. Her magic was enterprise. She took wool and silk from other states, and transformed it, and then found the markets for it.

The landed nobility who controlled Florence in its earliest days were bound to flounder before such persistent initiative. When the Guelf faction (supporters of the pope) and the Ghibelline faction (supporters of the Holy Roman Emperor) began to split the empire in the twelfth century, Florence was naturally on the side of the Guelfs. Whenever she tried to expand commercially, she was blocked along the country roads by the castles of the Teutonic nobles who levied impossible tolls or plundered her trains. There was something racial in the struggle too – the Etruscan or Romanic citizen against the Teutonic foreigner brought in by the emperor.

Yet the Guelf-Ghibelline feud was the beginning of Florence's success. She managed to draw the landed nobility into the city, partly through their increasing need for money and partly through the pleasures available inside the walls as people grew richer. At the same time, the guild system was developed as a protection for the new commercial interests, though for a time the nobles dominated the city by sheer brute force from their high towers. The city walls were enlarged in 1173. A constitution, probably her first, was produced, by which twelve consuls were to govern the city with the assistance of a hundred deputies elected by the guilds.

By the thirteenth century, her wool trade was booming. But no sooner was she strong – and this was typical of her history – than she was divided by new factions which again fell into the old Guelf-Ghibelline grouping. The guilds were now strong enough to begin quarrelling among themselves. The seven major guilds were strictly anti-noble, and expansionist. The fourteen lesser guilds, since they involved the consumer trades, were much less convinced that it was a good thing to eliminate the noble class, who stayed in their hotels and ate their food and ordered fine clothes from them. They preferred the noble round of tournaments, feasts and processions to the kind of prosperity that produced frantic constitution-making and sumptuary laws against luxury which discouraged the gay from spending. One tenth of the people was unemployed, and lived on pickings from noble self-indulgence. There lay the seed of the later explosion between labour on one side and capital on the other.

The starving, together with the so-called *ciompi* or wool-carders, had no political say in the city whatsoever. In a place in which people talked as much about freedom as the Florentines did, there was bound to be trouble sooner or later. The Guelf party for a long time shrugged off early signs of violence. Florence was, after all, the Guelf centre for northern and central Italy, which involved it in foreign alliances, and emergency armies which could always be used to keep the peace inside the city. The party had large revenues too.

But the more powerful the guilds became, the worse the danger of social revolution. In 1282 Florence's government was entirely in the hands of the major guilds, with the lesser guilds looking on. In 1293 new 'ordinances of justice' laid down that a noble entering a guild must practise a trade: it was the virtual end of the nobility.

In 1343 the constitution went through yet another of its almost annual reshufflings. The Guelf party was back in power, and at this point the richer families of the city, whether 'money-changers' (bankers) or merchants, were powerful enough to begin to assert themselves as single groups. Family-rule was perhaps the only political solution for Florence. No party based simply on shared commercial interests or Guelf sympathies or the guilds could find sufficient solidarity to govern well for long.

The family was indeed the one thing that survived the ups and downs of Florentine life. It has always been strong in Italy for reasons of necessity: no other institution has proved as durable. The family meant not simply parents and children but an army of relatives bearing the same name. Here the loyalty did not even have to be discussed. It was as natural as the day. Thus families became political parties because they were the only groups in which people really trusted each other. And these parties began to govern the city – or rather they began to fight each other constitutionally, which in Florence meant unconstitutionally.

Salvestro de' Medici became chief justice of the city in 1370 and again in 1378, probably under the protection of the Ricci family or the lesser guilds. He was certainly identified with the people, an identification which the Medici family always struggled to keep during the period of the republic. Salvestro set out to curb the Guelf party, especially in the matter of its so-called 'admonitions', namely decrees by which it could fix a crime on any citizen's shoulder.

The revolt of the *ciompi* in 1378 did the rest. Really the revolution spread downwards from Salvestro de' Medici: a strange situation had arisen in which the government had appealed for the people's support against the Guelf party. It gave the lesser guilds their chance to claim representation. It was the first disturbance to shake the city's trade. The result was that capital shrank, and unemployment grew. It forced the lesser guilds to unite with the greater, which gave capital its confidence back. The Guelf party now became virtually extinct as representative of a policy, yet the guilds too were politically superseded, so that the future lay between the rich and the poor, not the bigger or the lesser 'arts'. It was now the Florence of the great banking families. Through all its turmoils, the city had become perhaps the richest in the Italian peninsula, with the exception of the only other republic, Venice.

This did not mean, however, that there was peace. As Machiavelli wrote nearly a century and a half after the event, 'Sometimes the nobles of the people took arms, sometimes the major and sometimes the minor trades, and the lowest of the people. And it often happened that in different parts of the city all were at once in insurrection.' The new government fell in 1381, the greater guilds resumed control and the Albizzi family formed the oligarchy for which it had long been yearning. Maso degli Albizzi abolished the new guilds that had been formed and also reduced the power of the lesser ones. The city needed a strong hand not only to stop violence inside but to defend itself against the Duke of Milan, Gian Galeazzo Visconti, who was successfully closing Florence's trade routes in Lombardy. A new patriotism was stimulated.

About this time, we again hear of a Medici, still humble but less poor, though still very much identified with the people. In 1393 a deputation of lesser guildsmen waited on Vieri de' Medici to take up their cause, but he did not do so, probably because he saw that the city must have a period of firm government. Besides, Maso degli Albizzi was a genial man, combining compromise with severity in the most fascinating way. He may well have been a model for the Medici, and the chief reason why Vieri thought it unpolitic to rouse feeling against him. Like the Medici after him, he saw that it was better to befriend the great and flatter the poor than vice versa. Since money was the basis of the state, and not an armed and landed nobility, its shifts produced shocks that were felt in every class. The Medici were now a middle-class family, popular ever since Salvestro had been chief justice. He had been the founder-hero of the *ciompi* revolution, so that it was now difficult for the Medici name, however much wealth the family accumulated, to be suspected of reactionary attitudes.

Now Livorno (Leghorn) fell into Florence's hands, together with Prato, Pistoia, Volterra, Arezzo and Cortona. She now had an empire, and could secure safe roads for her trade to the sea. This period was in many ways a golden one for Florence. Pisa too yielded up its independence. There was a new grace in the people, a new luxury. And the city we know today took form, the 'new Athens' on the Arno.

The heart of Florence – the cathedral, the church of Santa Croce, the Signoria, with a cobweb of fascinating paved lanes between – was built in the last decade of the thirteenth century and the first two decades of the fourteenth. In that time too, Giotto painted his fresco-cycle at Padua. Cimabue had his studio in the area between Santa Croce and Sant' Ambrogio, then as now the city's sink of iniquity, with street-names like Malborghetto (or 'bad street'), now called Via de' Macci, and stone-inscriptions (still to be seen) banning whores. The *Divine Comedy* too was mostly completed in that time. Cimabue had done his work, now barely visible, at the San Francesco church in Assisi. During the following century Florence's cathedral got its bold cupola.

Florence has often been called the city of thought as well as of poetry: and the two, especially in the latter part of the fifteenth century, seemed always to be together, and to touch the frescoes, the sculpture and the music of the great houses and churches. This was the home of Leonardo da Vinci and Michelangelo, of Ghirlandaio and Filippo Lippi and Verrocchio and Donatello and Brunelleschi the architect. Its language had been made by Dante and Petrarch and Boccaccio.

The Medici were foremost among the patrons of the Renaissance, not

OPPOSITE The Medici bank in Milan, adapted from a palace given by Francesco Sforza. The houses opposite were demolished to improve the view.

uenti sei braccia pmo & ancora disopra una saletta amano mancha laquale e
lungha braccia uentidue & largha sette

Et ancora allo entrare della porta alzando gliocchi sie una loggia ncolonnette
dimarmo laquale risponde disopra acquella disotto nelcortile & della medesima
grandezza coe braccia uentiangi lungha & largha cinque laquale e dipinta inuer
de conlastoria disusanna nelparapetto dimanzi uoghono dipignere lemirtu cardi
nali Cosi disopra acqueste sie unaltra loggia laquale uiene aessere sopra iltreuo de
llamedesima larghezza & lunghezza della loggia detta laltezza non e tanto giu
to quella disotto & questa na due daogni canto lequali uengono acircunda
re tutto ilcortile datre parti elparapetto dinanzi & dicono cheuoghono dipig
nere liptaneti & segni colesti

Egli ancora certi ueroni liquali uanno dalla sala grande alle dette camere uno
dequali gliene che e braccia uenti & laltro e braccia dieci Coglione uno ilquale uiene
aessere sopra alla scala dibraccia quatordici

Aluro non accade dadire senon cheladetta casa e degnissima a Milano & ancora se
condo intendo lauoglono migliorare & ancora assai piu pche insono case aldirimpetto
della facciata lequali molto loccupano & pquesto lanno compare ognuarle interra a
cio chesia piu luminosa & piu bella pcheglisono molto propinque chenoneredo chesia
lastrada largha oltra otto braccia. Side non e dubbio cheogni uolta chelle dette case sa
ranno interra quella mosterra piu magnifica & molto piu bella ladetta facciata qua laquale
do sara hornata dicolori come dice uolerla fare none dubbo che a Milano none sa
ra unaltra simile considerato emolti hornamenti chella a maxime ladegna porta m
rmorea scolpita & intagliata degnissimamente come disopra dissi & ancora lentra
dessa e dignissima & maggiormente quando sara dipinta nelmodo chegia ragionami
insieme conpiggello portinari huomo dcomo & dabene elquale lui regge & guida tutto
eltraffico de canno a Milano colquale ebbi ragonamento diquello chedipignere saueua
Dissi chempareua douera dipignere nella uolta deldetto andiro della porta lestelle
fisse & nelle facciate daccanto sipuo fare lacosmogrofia & cosi daparte Tolommeo & altri
strologi Credo chesiquesta entrata sara bello expectaculo

ABOVE LEFT *Mercury* from *The Planets*, a series from about 1460, showing many fifteenth-century artistic pursuits.

ABOVE RIGHT *Jupiter* from *The Planets*. The scenes here are of falconry and hunting.

LEFT A terracotta roundel belonging to Florence's silk guild by Andrea della Robbia (1434–1528) in the oratory of Orsanmichele, Florence.

OPPOSITE Andrea del Verrocchio's bust of Lorenzo the Magnificent.

only because they were artistically inclined but because they saw the 'new' thought (which was in fact very old, being derived from ancient Greece and third-century AD Alexandria) and the 'new' art as the ingredients of a new civilisation which they hoped to make, in which there would be no war and no humbug. Florence was the seat of the first ecumenical council for the union of the Roman and Greek Orthodox Churches in 1438, not by a stroke of luck but by the persuasions of the Pope when the plague hit Ferrara, the intended site. That council brought Greeks to the homes of Florence: her citizens were struck by their visitors' brilliance in reasoning, and by a certain composure of mind that seemed to have been won from a different kind of knowledge, a greater knowledge, than that available to the Italian peninsula hitherto. It stimulated a frantic search for ancient manuscripts of every kind, and much Medici money went into this search, financing journeys throughout Asia to winkle out Chaldean, Hebrew, Alexandrian or Greek codices.

Florence became the richest city in Europe for its sense of an ancient past that had been closed for so long to the Christian mind: the Middle Ages began to look like a passage of darkness that had led from the Roman empire to the 'new' civilisation, or rather to the civilisation that was just round the corner (and seems still round the corner today).

The Renaissance was not a simple matter of art and thought, and graceful manners, and cities that enchanted the eye: violence was in it too. This did not abate with the invasion of Platonic thought: it increased. As the effects of the Renaissance spread in Europe, the violence increased there too, until it seemed that the more education, the more refinement and thought, the smaller the chances of peace. Behind every fresco, every commissioned sculpture for a palace garden, every dream of grandeur, whether it was Michelangelo's vision of a sculptured mountain or Leonardo's proposal to divert the course of the Arno river from its most favoured city, was a financial operation. The banking families – but principally the Medici – invested in a foreign war (at interest) or a foreign tapestry without seeing that in this lay a deadly contradiction. The Medici branches at Bruges, Geneva, Lyons and Antwerp were busy searching out choristers for the Pope and new flautists and paintings and manuscripts. And it was utterly baffling – it has baffled society since the fifteenth century – that worse and worse wars and persecutions accrued, not the expected civilisation. Therein lay the sadness of the Renaissance, the disillusion behind the talkative humanist movement which lit candles under Plato's bust (at least one Florentine suggested to the Pope that Plato should be canonised). If, for the modern visitor to Florence, there is something forbidding as well as captivating about the city, the reason must lie there, in a commercial enterprise that financed a bold bid for a new civilisation, indeed a really Christian civilisation for the first time, while underwriting a violence that at the same time made it impossible, and increasingly impossible. When society is geared to wealth, as

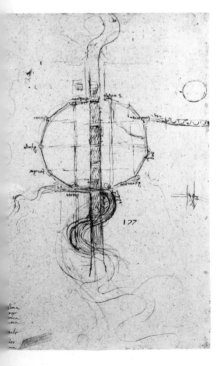

A diagrammatical drawing of Florence by Leonardo da Vinci. The River Arno runs in an arbitrary straight line through the city. This desire to rationalise nature was characteristic of Renaissance town planning and of Renaissance thought in general.

Guicciardini, Florence's historian of the republic, saw, it suffers the ups and downs of wealth, whose shifts make stable government impossible for long.

It was not only wool production that gave Florence her power in the world, or even the initiative of her citizens. A certain destiny was forced on her, and on the Medici who were by the fifteenth century identified with her. The Church was no longer the effective law-maker. Princes were no longer obedient servants of the Pope. They needed to be financed in their new ventures. And Florence, in the Medici, had the finances.

Of the other Italian states, however, Milan and Venice were both eager to lead, in addition to which the Papal States cut right across the peninsula and, at least before Venice started expanding, stretched from Ferrara in the north-east across the Romagna and Umbria down as far as Terracina south of Rome, where the territory of the other great Italian power, Naples, began. Florence was thus at the centre of formidable powers, protected only by mountains to the north and to the east, which was good from the military point of view but difficult for trade. She could easily become a battlefield for the other powers in conflict with each other. In Lorenzo's period, for a few frightening months, it happened. In this instance, he was at war with the pope. But even when Florence was at peace with everyone, she had to be careful to choose the right side when they went to war.

If anything underpinned her foreign policy, it was friendship with France. It always gave her a power of threat over other Italian states: the French were always ready to cross the Alps on behalf of one or other of their dynastic claims, to Piedmont, to Milan, to Naples. More than once, the King of France saved Lorenzo, as he saved his grandfather. On the other hand, Florence supported the Aragonese take-over of Naples because it kept France (with her royal claim to its throne) out of that kingdom: the King of Aragon was weak, and the unification of Castile and Aragon under Ferdinand and Isabella had not yet been dreamed of. Also, a Spaniard in Naples would help to keep an irritable Pope in check. He might twist the papal arm to divert attention from Florence's effort to get a port on the Mediterranean (hence her continual struggle with Pisa) and another on the Adriatic (hence her raids to the east). It was not for nothing that Medici rule lasted, apart from two brief interruptions, for the remarkable period of three centuries.

Florence under Cosimo

The motto of Giovanni di Averardo de' Medici's bank was *Col nome di Dio e di buon Ventura*, 'in the name of God and good fortune' – which could not have expressed better both the faith and the haunting doubt of the whole Renaissance enterprise. It was in the name of both that he educated his son Cosimo. At that time, permanent embassies in foreign capitals were not known: it was Ferdinand of Aragon who decided that they might be a good way of winning friends abroad, at the end of the fifteenth century. In the meantime, prominent citizens did the job, with a set mission, and they returned after a few weeks. Cosimo soon discovered that he was representing not only the city of Florence but his family interests as well. It was clear that when a foreign prince said 'Medici', he meant the city of Florence, and vice versa. A private loan from one of the Medici branches looked very much like an official loan from the Florentine state. It was equally clear that the man who convinced the people of Florence that in him lay a dual identity, both private and public, might control its government for always (*semper* being the family motto). Florence needed a monarchy: after all, this was what a ruling family, passing on its authority from one generation to the next, meant. But Florence dared not admit it, even to itself. The Medici understood this perfectly well, and Cosimo offered himself as the king who would never ask for a crown or even be seen in public.

When Giovanni di Averardo died, in 1429, Florence was in one of its periods of crisis, after years of war and defeat. 70,000 florins a month were being spent on military operations under the Albizzi family, who looked as if they were going to ask for a crown any day. Taxes were heavy, business was bad. Work was scarce. Twenty-five out of forty-three master craftsmen at work on Brunelleschi's cupola had to be laid off. Adding insult to injury, Rinaldo degli Albizzi reduced guild participation in civil affairs by half, and expropriated confraternity property. In 1433 Cosimo led the opposition to this (always careful to espouse the people's cause when it was politic to do so) and found himself under arrest in the Signoria, having been called there for his 'advice'. It is said that only a number of bribes in the right direction saved his life. But more likely than this, as the factor which decided Rinaldo to banish him instead of strangling him, was the close interest taken in his welfare by France, Venice and the Pope. Cosimo was in Venice as an exile for a year (1433), living much like a foreign prince, honoured and fêted wherever he went. During his absence, popular feeling inside Florence ran high, and the big families began to fear that, with Milanese help,

ABOVE Portrait of Cosimo de'
Medici, Lorenzo's grandfather,
by Bronzino (1503–72).
Cosimo received the
posthumous title of *Pater
Patriae* or Father of the
Fatherland. A man of ascetic
taste, he was the first Medici
to concentrate Florence's
political affairs entirely in
Medici hands, while
controlling with minute
attention the family's banks in
every part of Europe.

BELOW Giovanni and Piero de'
Medici, Lorenzo's elder sons,
in a fresco by Domenico
Ghirlandaio (1451–1525) in the
church of S. Trinità in
Florence. Giovanni became
Pope Leo X, while Piero's
errors after Lorenzo's death
brought to an end the
republican period of Medici
rule.

Rinaldo would get that crown. Behind his back, Pope Eugenius IV (at the time a guest of the Albizzi family) convinced the *signori* that Cosimo must be recalled and Rinaldo thrown out. When Cosimo returned, he lent the Signoria vast sums of money, and gradually put the city back on its feet. With more justice than a French king, he could have said '*l'état, c'est moi*'. He did not expect to be paid back, but nothing could have been a better investment. His palace (not yet the one in Via Larga) became a second town hall. He began to entertain foreign dignitaries. He paid the bills for housing the Byzantine Emperor, John Palaeologos, and his enormous retinue, during the ecumenical council of 1438. When the later Pope Pius II paid Florence a visit, he staged a joust, a ball at the Mercato Nuovo and a hunt with lions, wolves and wild boars in the well-barricaded Piazza della Signoria. It was clear that of all Florentines, he was a good man to get to know.

Yet he was more than the state, by being nothing more than a citizen. He was no less humble than before. He lived in no greater splendour. He was loved for being the very spirit of Florence. Pius II described him as a man of fine physique and more than average height, with a mild expres-

The Palazzo Medici in Via Cavour, then the Via Larga, Florence. It was begun in 1444 by the architect Michelozzo, under Cosimo de' Medici. Cosimo spent only the last five years of his life there, never feeling really at home since the vast palace was more a party headquarters than a private residence. Its furnishings were completed by Cosimo's son Piero.

sion and manner of speech, more cultured than merchants usually are, and with some knowledge of Greek. His mind was alert and keen, his spirit neither brave nor cowardly. He took hard work easily, and often passed a night without sleep. Nothing went on in Italy that he did not know about, and little in the rest of Europe that one of his banks did not fully inform him about. His branches at Milan, Venice, Pisa, Rome, Avignon, Lyons, Geneva, Bruges and London were now firmly respectable institutions which avoided risky speculations.

The vast Palazzo Medici was begun in 1444 and he spent only the last five years of his life there. He was never really happy there, partly because it was a business and party headquarters, partly because he preferred to be near his vines and olives at his country seat in Careggi. Not even his son Giovanni's splendid new villa at Fiesole pleased him as much as the simple Careggi house, because, he said, his son's windows looked over Florence, while his own looked over miles of Medici property. Yet the Palazzo Medici is simple and not strikingly neo-classical. Its first two storeys are clothed in a stout and forbidding wall of rough blocks of stone, in the *rustica* style. Only above this is the palazzo clearly fifteenth-century, but even here the classical emphasis is not great. The Middle Ages have been rejected, yet with some regret: and the result is something of a cloistral atmosphere, endowed with wealth and a touch of arrogance.

The 'Medici area' behind the cathedral, consisting of Palazzo Medici (now Riccardi-Medici, and the seat of the Prefecture), the churches of San Lorenzo and San Marco, with the university, is not the most pleasant part of Florence. The Via Cavour in which the *palazzo* stands must have been as broad as it is now, its name being 'broad street'. The *Studio Generale*, as the university was first called when it came into being in 1321, had failed to attract Petrarch when he was offered the chancellorship (once in 1351 and again in 1356), perhaps because its standards were

The Annunciation, by Fra' Filippo Lippi (c. 1406–69), an overdoor from the Palazzo Medici. The three feathers in a diamond ring, shown beneath the lilies, were a device of the Medici family. Together with Donatello, Castagno, Fra' Angelico and Benozzo Gozzoli, Fra' Filippo was honoured and patronised by Cosimo de' Medici, Lorenzo's father.

43

The interior of San Lorenzo, the 'Medici church'. It was built between 1419 and 1469 on a design by Filippo Brunelleschi (1377–1446), and was Florence's first church in the new style of the Renaissance. Its building was largely under the control of the Medici family. Financial troubles interrupted work until 1442, when Cosimo gave the city 40,000 florins to complete the nave.

not high. So the university declined before it had really begun, almost as if Florence were too intelligent for it to be necessary. As for San Lorenzo, its building was an enterprise inherited from Giovanni di Averardo, but that too was interrupted until finally Cosimo lent the city 40,000 florins to pay for the nave. In the case of San Marco too, he underwrote the debt, after Pope Eugenius IV had allowed the Dominican friars of Fiesole to take it over.

44

Even Cosimo's books were those of a man of ascetic taste. In manuscript collecting he was the rival of any other of Florence's great men. Vespasiano da Bisticci the bookseller, who had a team of scribes under him to copy manuscripts which Cosimo could borrow but not buy, said that his master spent more on manuscripts than he did on his palace. While the ecumenical council was meeting, Bisticci's team was forty-five strong, and they copied out over two hundred codices. The stimulus these gave to Florentine thought, together with the presence of men like George Gemistos Plethon, the Greek delegate from Trebizond, were the real achievements of the council, whose proclamation of union between the two Churches lasted just about a year, to be followed fourteen years later by the collapse of Constantinople under the Turks.

In spite of the search for manuscripts and the sense among the city's most learned men (which meant its chancellors and ambassadors) that the doors were now open to the ancient world, the emphasis was still on the Church, on monastic studies and the medieval doctrine of renunciation as almost the basis of life. This was very strong in Cosimo, and it may account for the fact that the 'Medici area' of Florence, conceived by Giovanni and completed by him, has a perplexing disharmony, between the darkly cloistral and the blatantly commercial, quite distinct from the rest of the city. Cosimo himself would spend hours in silent meditation in his study at Careggi, and he once wrote to his favourite Marsilio Ficino, in whose hands he had placed the new 'Platonic Academy', that he went to his estate to improve not his fields but himself, and that Plato's works constituted the best vehicle for self-improvement. This did not mean a conscious departure from Christian feeling, for the Platonists saw Greek thought as a means of illuminating Christ's teaching, much as Plotinus and the Alexandrian thinkers of the third century AD had seen it. Cosimo was looking for happiness ('There is no employment to which I so ardently devote myself as to find out the true road to happiness') but in a mystical sense. Something had gone wrong. Most men were aware of that. The faith of earlier times might seem crude in the light of Greek thought, but it had been robust. The Renaissance was a great outburst of confidence which concealed (perhaps was caused by) great tremors of doubt. The conflict was even deeper in Lorenzo.

Lorenzo was nine when a political crisis nearly sent his grandfather into exile a second time, in 1458. Cosimo had learned from the period of his banishment that Florence's recovery had to be master-minded. No one wanted to go back to the old days of unemployment and defeat. He felt also that it gave him the chance to tighten the government towards the Medici interest. However, a constitutionalist movement started and spread inside the Medici party. It even managed to monopolise the government, and insisted on a *Balìa* or committee of constitutional reform. On the other hand, the big commercial families like the Strozzi and the Pitti soon began to realise that only Cosimo stood between them and the constitutionalists, almost as their protector. But Cosimo would not risk his popularity by coming forward to sponsor them. We have to realise that even now he was not the acknowledged head of anything. He could quite honestly have said that he was only a simple merchant, and had nothing to do with politics, though a number of people did come to his house every day for advice. It was perhaps the most subtle and inviolable dictatorship ever devised.

Cosimo therefore gave his support to Luca Pitti, a headstrong creature who could be relied on to curb the new liberalism. In July, as chief justice, Pitti proposed that the boxes of nominated candidates for the Signoria should be burned, and the names of the new *signori* drawn by hand. He was defeated, so he called a *parlamento*, a mass gathering in the main square. The people shouted 'yes' to another 'committee of reform', and this filled the boxes of nomination with Medici names for the next five years.

This one act did more to put the Medici family in the public saddle for the next fifty or so years than anything else. From that time, Cosimo was seldom in the public eye. He was broken by gout and grief over the death of his favourite son, Giovanni, in 1463. In any case, his complete mastery of the situation made frequent appearances both unnecessary and unwise. The hero of the *coup d'état* was Luca Pitti, Cosimo's puppet.

Lorenzo grew up watching his grandfather. He saw an ideal head of family, who always preached sympathy and affection to the young. A family must hold together in love. that was what Cosimo always maintained, and why he never made a will. He was a grave man, rather silent, yet witty too. He had a tiny room in St Mark's convent in which he spent hours of his time to escape the bustle of his own home, mostly talking with Antonino, the city's archbishop. He was most himself at ease among the artists of his time and the literary men. Yet, apparently without effort, he made Florence one of the great states of Italy, on a level with Naples, Rome, Milan and Venice.

Cosimo had not long to live. On 26 July 1464, Piero wrote to his sons, in the intimate and unhurried style of the time:

I wrote to you the day before yesterday and told you how Cosimo had worsened, then it seemed to me that he was declining, and so it seemed to him too, so much that by Tuesday he only wanted Monna Contessina [his wife] and myself in the room. He began to recount his whole life, then he talked about the government of the city, and about the factions, from that to the management of the family possessions and house, and then about the two of you, exhorting me, as you are both so well-gifted, to bring you up well, so that some of the burden might be lifted from my shoulders, adding that two things pained him, the first that he had not done all he had wanted to and could have done in life, and the second that, since I am frail in health, he was leaving me with such cares. . . . And he said everything with such composure and prudence, and in such a great spirit, that it was a marvel to see. . . . And you must take an example from this, for you are both young, and must now take your portion of the burden, because Messer Domenedio [literally 'Mr Lord God'] disposes. And please take account of the fact that you are men now, though still boys, as the present situation requires, for your benefit and good, because the time has come for you to gain experience, and live in fear of God, and keep good cheer. I will let you know what happens with Cosimo. We are expecting a doctor from Milan to arrive any minute, but I have more faith in Messer Domenedio than in others. Nothing more at present. Ghareggi, 26 July 1464.

Part One

Florence under Piero, 1464-69

Cosimo died a few days later. Piero took over the 'succession', but without his two young sons he would have been helpless. Lorenzo's public life began, though he was only sixteen. Piero managed Florence's affairs as best he could from Careggi, bedridden with gout, while Lorenzo and Giuliano (six years younger than Lorenzo), both of them brilliant and popular, ran the Medici party in town. Already Lorenzo had learned enough from his grandfather to be an able, though of course not yet a prudent, politician. He had accompanied his father and Cosimo everywhere and had been included in all the important party discussions. He had sat with his family at the great banquets, and at the more useful private dinner parties. He was used to the company of princes and ambassadors.

He owed much to his mother, Lucrezia Tornabuoni, of whom Cosimo

A sixteenth-century portrait of Giovanni di Cosimo de' Medici by Angelo Bronzino. Giovanni was brought up by Cosimo as his successor in the rule of Florence, since his eldest son Piero was an invalid, but he died young.

had once said, with little justice to his son, 'She is the only man in the house.' Her family had abandoned its noble status to enter politics. Her grandfather had attached himself to the Medici party, and the two families had been close ever since. She was a devout woman, and wrote some of the finest hymns, or *laudi*, in the Italian language, but she had nothing of the prig about her. She was Lorenzo's ablest adviser, and she bolstered the Medici popularity with endowments in the right places, and dowries to needy girls.

Lorenzo threw himself into learning as he did into horse-riding and horse-breeding (he had a passion for thoroughbreds) – with a zest that captivated everyone round him. His tutor, Gentile Becchi, later Bishop of Arezzo, came from Urbino, where the Court under Federigo da Montefeltro achieved a refinement of life hardly paralleled in the rest of the peninsula. He could not have had a more civilising background. Becchi was an ardent Latinist. As to Greek, Lorenzo learned this from a native in the language, the famous Johannis Argyropoulos, a refugee from the ruin of the Greek empire. Aristotle and Plato came to him this way, as if from the land of Greece itself. It meant that he always approached the classics spontaneously, and wrote Latin as if it were a living

Lorenzo's father, Piero de' Medici by Mino da Fiesole (1429–84). Piero governed Florence for only five years, from 1464. Although he died of gout, the family disease, when he was only fifty-three, he was instrumental in preparing the public mind for Lorenzo's acceptance as the city's 'prince'.

RIGHT Giovanni di Cosimo de'
Medici (1421–63) by Mino da
Fiesole (1429–84). His sudden
death at the early age of
forty-two was a great blow to
the Medici hopes.

OPPOSITE Botticelli's *Madonna
of the Magnificat*, painted in
1465 for Piero de' Medici,
showing Lorenzo (with
inkstand) and his brother
Giuliano.

BELOW *The Birth of John the
Baptist*, a fresco by Domenico
Ghirlandaio in the church of
S. Maria Novella. The third
lady on the right is Lucrezia
Tornabuoni, Lorenzo's
mother.

IVLIANVS MED. PETRI F. COSMI P.P. NEP.

tongue. His thinking, in the Greek tradition, was never forced, as it was among so many of the Platonic devotees who had never read an original word of Plato. His other teachers (rather friends of the family) were Marsilio Ficino, his grandfather's guide and solace in classical learning, who translated Plato into Latin, and Cristofero Landino, who wrote a long commentary on the *Divine Comedy* and translated Aristotle.

Lorenzo adored the rest of his family – his brother Giuliano, tall and much more handsome than himself, with curling black hair, who was fêted wherever he went. His sisters were equally attractive. Bianca was already married to Guglielmo Pazzi, while the younger Nannina, pious like her mother, married Bernardo Rucellai later, in 1466. Both the Pazzi and the Rucellai were prominent families, close to the Medici, though the Pazzi were to have their names and most of their persons expunged from memory twenty years or so later. The Pazzi were noblemen who had moved to Florence, while the Rucellai, like the Medici, had made their way up by trade, making a fortune in *oricello*, a new purple dye.

It was not an easy period for the Medici interest, least of all for Piero. Florence was going through one of her sudden financial crises. There was a crop of unexplained bankruptcies which ricochetted down through society. The Partini brothers went broke, then Ludovico Strozzi, Lorenzo d'Ilarione Ilarioni (the most spectacular crash of all, with 160,000 florins, nearly £7 million, owing – he was the grandson of the Medici's general manager of 1420 to 1438), and a number of smaller firms, the Maestro Cristofani, the Baldesi, the Banchi, the Zorzi. The Salviati company was in difficulties, though here an advance of 12,000 florins from the Medici bank saved the day. These things happened immediately after Cosimo's death, and naturally people thought, or pretended to think, that they had something to do with Piero, though he was hardly in the saddle.

Also, Piero's 'succession' to the non-existent throne excited not only resentment but surprise in the great families. It had much to do with the depression. So the Medici *were* a dynasty after all! Agnolo Acciaiuoli, who had been exiled to Venice with Cosimo, was now an opponent of the Medici party, after a number of family setbacks which he attributed to Cosimo, among them the fact that his son did not get the archbishopric of Pisa. Also, the Rucellai marriage with Nannina robbed him of the closer connection with the Medici which he coveted. He became a conspirator with three other men, Niccolò Soderini, Diotisalvi Neroni and the prominent Luca Pitti.

Soderini's father had been hanged for forging documents to prove his own legitimacy. The family had blamed his death on the Albizzi and had gone over to the Medici party (Piero's wife's sister had married Tommaso Soderini). But Niccolò was a man of fire, though it was easy to put the fire out. He had ambitions and ideals, and mixed the two in such an unpalatable way that no one really understood what he was at. His

brother, who kept his distance during the conspiracy, prophesied that he would 'enter like a lion and go out like a lamb', and this was precisely what he did. As to Diotisalvi Neroni, he was the brains of the group. Through Medici influence, his brother had become archbishop of Florence. The families had been so close that Cosimo had advised Piero to put all his confidence in Diotisalvi. Luca Pitti, whose wealth stood second only to that of the Medici, was the oldest of the conspirators, and ought to have known better. Not that any of them was young. It was Lorenzo de' Medici who got around Florence and influenced young minds. They were too old for violence, but violence was the only way open to them after they had tried unsuccessfully to influence the *gonfalonieri* and the councils against Piero.

It is said that Neroni cunningly advised Piero, as a first step to his downfall, to call in all Medici debts, a quite usual procedure on the death of a principal, but a tricky thing to do at this moment, with so many business-men in trouble. Piero was obliged by the bankrupt state of the times to inspect the Medici books thoroughly for long-standing debts, and to call in what he could. The London branch of the bank was in trouble, largely through its loans to Edward IV which remained unpaid. He ordered the Milan branch to reduce its loans to the Sforza family. He wound up the Venice branch, which was not doing good business. What seems probable is that Neroni encouraged his policy of retraction for his

OPPOSITE A detail from Benozzo Gozzoli's *The Journey of the Magi*. This shows Lorenzo's three sisters, Nannina, Bianca and Maria between the ages of twelve and fourteen.

BELOW The vast Pitti palace built by Luca Pitti to outshine the Medici palace on the other side of the river.

own ends, seeing that it would involve unpopularity. But Piero could not have been blind to this result, on his side.

Things did not look good for the Medici party. It was divided between the 'Mountain' (those who supported Pitti on his Bóboli hill) and the 'Plain' (down at Via Larga). Piero lost a constitutional battle over the ballot boxes. Choosing magistrates by lot was at the moment too popular a method to be turned down. It meant the temporary end of Medici control in the Signoria, and the Signoria for October was favourable to the 'Mountain'.

Niccolò Soderini was made chief justice. He did a great deal of talking and even summoned five hundred prominent citizens to the *palazzo* for a long talking-to about the current situation. It was a failure. No one seemed to want his revolution. He proposed that the council of one hundred be abolished. That would really have meant the end of the Medici. But again no one was with him. He tried to get himself knighted but the council of the *comune* did not want to know about that either. He then went out like a lamb, as his brother had promised. Medici supporters lit bonfires in the main square. They wrote the words 'NINE FOOLS ARE OUT' on the walls before dawn, the nine being Acciaiuoli and his two sons, Neroni and two of his brothers, Niccolò Soderini with his son Geri, and Luca Pitti. It was not the end of trouble, only a lull. The violence was yet to come. In the meantime, Soderini paraded the streets with a bodyguard, hoping to give the impression that his life was in danger.

Meanwhile, Piero went on with the quiet work of patronage which he had inherited from his father. He furnished the town *palazzo* completely. The painters had for a long time been closer to him than to the busy and preoccupied Cosimo. Domenico Veneziano and Fra' Filippo Lippi had in any case always written to him with their requests, not to the 'old one'. He loved the old courtly style of painting, and when the time came for Benozzo Gozzoli to paint the tiny Medici chapel in the Via Larga

The lily of the *comune* of Florence, from a fifteenth-century building.

house Piero asked him to follow the 'antique' style of Gentile da Fabriano and Fra' Angelico. This produced the *Journey of the Magi* (1459), seen as a long procession of visiting Greeks and eminent Florentines, on the occasion of the ecumenical council twenty-one years before. The last Greek emperor was there, and Lorenzo at the age of ten as the youngest of the holy kings, looking proud and angelic in glittering jewel-studded mail over a brocaded jacket. His three sisters, Maria, Nannina and Bianca, are seen together: they were between twelve and fourteen years old when Benozzo painted them. It is a delicate and lyrical fresco to the glory of God and the Medici, and a certain radiant hope centres on the figure of the young Lorenzo, riding almost alone. His prominent jaw and large nose are missing but the sweetness and musing tenderness, captured in idealised features, are more true to the man than any more lifelike portrait has conveyed.

Piero sent him on his first important diplomatic mission in April 1465. It was to Pisa to meet Don Federigo of Aragon, son of the King of Naples. Federigo was escorting Ippolita Sforza (Francesco's daughter) back to Naples to marry his brother Alfonso, Duke of Calabria. From the

60

moment he and Lorenzo met, they were close friends, and the intimacy lasted all their lives. They talked about poetry, and Federigo asked Lorenzo what Italian poetry he liked best and would advise a virtual foreigner to read. Lorenzo promised to send him a manuscript collection and did so the following year. He added some poems of his own, sonnets and songs, with a few prefatory lines for Federigo himself.

Florence hated Federigo when he reached the city with his retinue and six hundred horse a few days later. His Court was in mourning for the late Queen of Naples. That was boring enough for a city that liked a good time. But also Spanish pride prevented him from dismounting from his horse at the Signoria. It was the kind of thing for which Florentines hated princes. But it was a personal success for Lorenzo, who shone at Federigo's side as a jewel of youthful courtesy and tact. As it turned out, his friendship with the Neapolitan House saved Florence and his own life, not to say the Medici dynasty, some years later.

He accompanied the party to Milan for the ensuing celebration, together with one of the would-be conspirators against his father, Diotisalvi Neroni, who was representing the state of Florence, and his brother-in-law Guglielmo Pazzi. Neroni was knighted by the Duke of Milan who, despite the fact that he owed his dukedom to Medici money, thought that Neroni might very well push Piero out.

As far as Piero was concerned, this journey was the real test of Lorenzo's ability, and he wrote him a long letter in which he advised him not to stint on entertainment, but on the other hand not to try to outshine his hosts. He must remember to be a man in word and deed, not a boy, since this journey would decide whether he was to be sent on other missions. Also, Lorenzo should tell Guglielmo de' Pazzi 'not to forget us altogether, and you too do not give so much thought to the festivities that you forget your own home. You must come back a few days before the wedding party arrives here, for I shall have the princess in the house, and without you and Guglielmo I shall be as a man without hands.'

Already, Lorenzo was being noticed and talked about. He rarely said a word too much, while being perfectly natural and spontaneous. With learned men, he was neither over-awed nor casual, at a time when ambassadors and chancellors and chamberlains were often well-known scholars too. In the spring of 1466, he was employed on a more important mission, on which much could depend. Piero sent him to Rome, nominally to discuss alum mines which were in papal hands. Pope Pius II had died a few days after Cosimo, and the new man was Paul II, one of the most arrogant popes who ever lived.

During the fifteenth century, alum was a most important product. It was used for glassmaking, tanning and – here lay Florence's interest in the mineral – cleaning wool, as well as for fixing dyes. There being no adequate substitute for alum, merchants and princes tended to scramble for ownership of the mines. Until 1455, when the Turks drove them out,

OPPOSITE A detail from the *Confirmation of the Rule*, a fresco from S. Trinità, Florence, by Domenico Ghirlandaio with portraits of Antonio Pucci, Lorenzo de' Medici, Stefano di Giovanni Sassetta the painter, and his son.

A medal from 1441 by Pisanello (*c.* 1395–1455) showing Filippo Maria Visconti, Duke of Milan.

the Genoese had controlled the richest alum deposits in existence, those near Smyrna. The Turks now demanded high prices, and the result was that Christian princes found themselves financing their worst enemy. There was a tiny amount of alum at Ischia, but the situation changed when a Paduan discovered rich quantities at Tolfe, near Civitavecchia. There was great joy at the Vatican, and in September 1462 Pope Pius IV had ratified an agreement with the new, so-called *Societas Aluminum*. This was renewed in 1465. Within a year of the new agreement, the Medici bank had become a partner in the firm, with a quarter of the equity. The deal was signed in April 1466, and this was the ostensible reason for Lorenzo's visit. The new Pope was in as friendly a mood towards Florence as possible in view of her recent support of Ruberto Malatesta of Rimini against his design to annex that state as a papal possession. Later there developed bitter hostility between Pope Paul and the Medici, not least because of the Pope's dislike of extreme neo-platonists.

Lorenzo had a tough job, therefore, but acquitted himself well, especially as on arrival he heard of the death of Francesco Sforza. Though Sforza had reigned for sixteen years, his son had no official title to the duchy of Milan. There was a further complication in that this son was away fighting the Duke of Bourbon in France.

Piero showed immediate energy and sent a letter to Lorenzo post haste. It was dated 15 March, from Careggi: 'I find myself in such affliction and distress over the sad and unfortunate death of His Highness the Duke of Milan that I hardly know where I am. You can imagine what importance, public and private, this has. . . . There are letters from Milan of the 9th and 10th which I am enclosing so that you will understand how things are. . . . I have also written to His Holiness.' He advised Lorenzo to give up *'sonare d'instrumenti o canti e balli, o simili altre cose d'allegrezza'* ('playing of instruments or songs and dances, or other similar shows of gaiety'), and to bear himself like a man, and to discuss matters only with Giovanni Tornabuoni, his uncle, and Medici bank-manager in Rome, and the young Malatesta who was also there. Lorenzo's job was to let the Pope know that Piero had pledged himself to uphold the Sforza dynasty, and to see that the succession passed to Francesco's widow and sons. After some time. Lorenzo was able to write to him that the Pope too wanted peace in that area, and seemed to bear towards him the utmost respect and friendliness.

Florence would have remained at peace had it not been for Diotisalvi Neroni, who was used to travelling about Italy and discussing Medici fortunes with other powers such as Venice. It was clear that he was planning a *coup d'état* with foreign aid, at least with that of Ferrara. The opposition to Piero was growing every day with the commercial distress. The conspirators also had it in mind that Piero was possibly too weak to govern, and his children too young. The thing had to be done as soon as

possible, since the constitutional intrigue to get rid of him had failed.

Diotisalvi knew that he had Venice behind him, for Venice hoped that through him Florentine foreign policy would switch back to its old pre-Cosimo orientation and become anti-Milanese once more. The unpopularity of the new Milanese connection in Florence also gave them more hope than there was. Diotisalvi tried to win over King Ferrante, Alfonso's successor in Naples. If that failed, he determined to set the French on Ferrante, in the person of the son of King René of Anjou, for the Anjou claim to Naples was still very much alive. Diotisalvi failed in all his missions. It perhaps took more than his powers, and a lifetime of training, to reach Lorenzo de' Medici's know-how in politics, which seemed almost a natural function of his mind.

A panel from a fifteenth-century chest depicting the wedding ceremony between Boccaccio Adimari and Lisa Ricasoli, both members of prominent Florentine families.

The Venetians did not give Diotisalvi aid after all, being too busy with the Turks in their own imperial waters. In the other states of Italy, the Medici had far too much influence. Lorenzo was sent on a quick visit to Naples, where he was enthusiastically received, and had a chance of seeing Federigo again.

At this point, the Ferrarese army under Borso d'Este made a tell-tale move towards Pistoia just outside Florence. It was now obvious to everyone that Neroni and his party were planning a *coup d'état* with the Ferrarese in support. Piero was still bedridden at Careggi, but on 23 August 1466 had himself carried to Florence. The 'Mountain' seemed determined to kill him. They placed an ambush near the Badìa at Fiesole, which Piero's litter had to pass on its way to the Porta Faenza. But Lorenzo was riding in advance. Some ill-looking men approached his group and asked him whether Piero was following. He replied that he was and then, with remarkable presence of mind for a gay youth of seventeen, sent back a messenger to his father advising him to enter the city by another gate. This is not quite an authenticated story, but it seems probable. The chief objection to it is that the road by the Badìa to the Faenza gate is not the straightest road from Careggi, which is well to the west of it. But Piero may have taken the alternative road to mislead conspirators, and they may have heard of his new route too late, whence the uncertainty of the ill-looking men.

We do know that the Ferrarese were lying in wait at Pistoia. That day armed peasants were brought into the city to defend the Medici party. The Signoria was rather favourable to the 'Mountain', though it was obliged to send a reconnaissance group to Pistoia to find out what the Ferrarese were up to. That night the Medici palace was barricaded. Armed peasants swarmed around it. On the other side of the river, there were two hundred armed men milling around outside the Pitti palace. It looked like civil war. Niccolò Soderini was for an outright attack on the Medici palace, and then forcible occupation of the Signoria. Others wanted to set fire to all the houses in the 'Plain' area. This for Neroni was going too far – since his own house was in the 'Plain'. More sober elements in the party prevailed, pointing out that if there was that sort of violence, another *ciompi*-style revolution might ensue. In other words. the conspirators lost heart and got in each other's way. Agnolo Acciaiuoli hated any kind of lawlessness, and preferred even the Medici to mob-rule. All these men were well settled in life, and had too much to lose from changes which they felt they wanted, without knowing precisely how they would rule in the place of the Medici. Luca Pitti, the most prominent citizen of them all, wavered and looked glum.

Morale at the Medici palace was much higher. The younger men wanted to attack the Pitti palace, but Piero quashed any such idea. Like all good Medici, he worked through the law and not violence, while it was still possible. In the meantime, Milanese troops, called to Florence after Piero's appeal to the Sforza family, had reached the outskirts of the city. From Volterra alone, a column of four hundred marched in. The Medici men got hold of the ballot boxes, fixed the names and produced a new Signoria favourable to themselves. That was precisely five days after Piero had moved to Florence, on 28 August.

The outgoing officials asked for a meeting with the Medici party, and Piero sent Lorenzo and Giuliano along to do the talking. The moment they got to the Signoria, it was obvious that no one wanted a fight. Everything was affability. The two sides swore to lay down their arms, and embraced warmly on the spot. Luca Pitti, falling over himself to retain the look of a respectable citizen, went in company with other members of his party to Piero's bedside. There was some talk of a forth-coming marriage involving the Medici and Pitti families. Luca Pitti stayed on in the bedroom after his men left, together with Lorenzo and Giuliano. They talked for some time about the absurdity of being enemies, and the future that would be an all-the-better peace.

Luca left with tears in his eyes. But he had not been outside the palace for many hours when Niccolò Soderini managed to persuade him that they must have one more try, and violence was the only way. Luca was agreeable to trying again but still adamant against violence. Meanwhile, the new Signoria began its sittings. By 1 September the Medici party was safe again. The new chief justice was Ruberto Lioni, a man of good sense and proven loyalty to Piero. The next day the Signoria bell tolled for a *parlamento*. The hired and watched crowd granted a *Balìa* or committee of reform for four months. On the fifth day of September, the *Balìa* decided by 199 votes to seventy-seven that emergency authority must be given to the *Podestà* (or captain) for at least five years, and to the so-called Eight of Watch and Ward (a kind of Ministry of the Interior) for ten years. This meant, when spelled out in hard power-terms, that the Medici were safe for the next ten years, and could officially call on armed support to prove it.

The conspirators were now at Piero's mercy. Lorenzo, his son, once said that 'Only he knows how to conquer who can forgive.' He had been taught that by his father and grandfather before him. Piero ordered Niccolò Soderini and his sons to Provence, where they already had good friends who might by now have overturned the state of Naples had Pitti's influence been greater. Agnolo Acciaiuoli was to be exiled to Barletta in the south-east, but they had already fled. Piero would prob-ably have pardoned Acciaiuoli, whose reluctance to say boo to a goose he knew about. Neroni had fled to Rome. That family never lifted its head again. Lucca Pitti remained in Florence, unpunished, but all Florence turned its back on him and his party. Workmen refused to continue work on his great house. The Medici disowned the proposed marriage between Lorenzo and one of the Pitti daughters. She had to marry Lorenzo's uncle, Giovanni Tornabuoni, instead, which was still a very good match. Businessmen who had advanced money for the Pitti palace in the form of gifts now demanded it back. Piero showed no vindictiveness, which endeared him to all the city. He even went out of his way to mitigate any sense of harshness by recalling some old families like the Strozzi from their exile.

Diotisalvi Neroni, on the other hand, was by no means in a forgiving or forgetting mood. He went to Venice, where he had confidential talks with the *condottiere* Bartolomeo Colleone, who was also Venice's captain-general. Borso d'Este, the Ferrarese leader, decided to give the exiles fourteen hundred horse. In the meantime, Florence had alerted Milan and Naples, who sent troops to her support. Galeazzo Maria Sforza was now Duke of Milan. His troops joined up with those of King Ferrante in the Romagna. As for the Florentine army, a great Neapolitan noble, Ruberto San Severino, was its commander. Count Federigo of

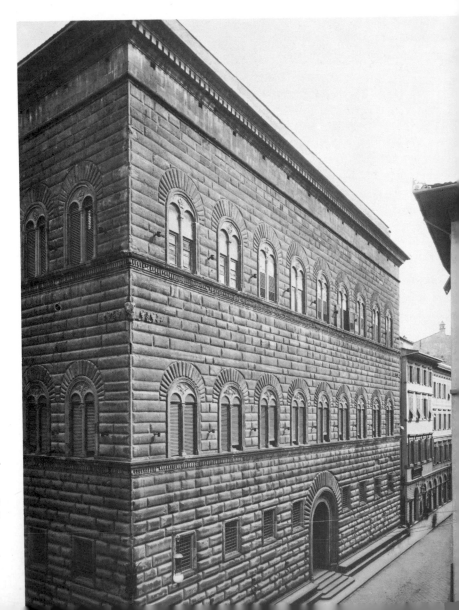

The Palazzo Strozzi was begun in 1489, probably on a design by Giuliano da Sangallo. The walls are set with gigantic blocks of stone in the aggressively grand 'rustic' style of the time, which imitated the Etruscan wall.

Urbino was commander-in-chief of the combined armies. It was lucky for Florence that the conspiratorial conflict was now being fought out in battle and far from the city. At that time it was difficult to get hurt in war. Mercenary captains hated to attack each other, and took care to take prisoners (their colleagues, after all) instead of killing. It meant that life could go on in Florence as if nothing had happened. On the other hand, a prolonged state of war, however choreographic, closed her trade routes, and she soon began urging the Duke of Milan to press an attack home, instead of allowing Federigo of Urbino and Bartolomeo Colleone to continue their dance-improvisations in the old style. Lorenzo did not visit headquarters. Besides having little interest in war, like a good Florentine, he more and more had to assume control in the city in his father's stead.

At last, Bartolomeo Colleone was defeated, after a brisk attack by Federigo of Urbino. The war was over by the spring of 1468. The Pope was a disappointed man. It was not only papal power politics that stood between him and the Medici. He was a Venetian, too, and there is no doubt that he played a leading role in this last attempt to root them out and substitute a government in Florence that would be favourable to himself and the Venetian republic. Paul II was obliged to abandon the services of Colleone, who wanted to lead the imminent attack on the Turks as commander-in-chief not only of the Venetian mercenaries but of the whole army. He abandoned the Florentine exiles too. Inside Florence, orders were given for the confiscation of the exiles' property, since they had broken bounds. Even so, Soderini's son Tommaso and Acciaiuoli's son Donato were left with something, since they had continued to serve Florence as ambassadors.

In the meantime, Lorenzo had found another friend equal to Federigo, this time a woman and Federigo's sister-in-law, Ippolita Sforza, now Duchess of Calabria, whom Lorenzo had met for the first time at Pisa during her wedding preparations. Whether there was more than platonic love between them we do not know, but we do know that Plato figured in nearly all their conversations, and that the new civilisation which it was every humanist's hope to see emerge from the scholastic ashes of the Middle Ages was already realised in them both. After her two months' stay at Siena she returned with her husband Alfonso to Florence, which became his winter quarters for the war against the exiles. His stay was mostly at the expense of the Medici.

The friendship with Naples, now equally a key to Florentine policy as that with Milan, was very much the personal work of Lorenzo. King Ferrante wrote to him in September 1466, not long after his visit:

Magnifice vir amice noster carissime [Your Magnificence, our most dear friend] we love you both for your own qualities and your family merits and heritage. But in the manly prudence and courage with which you have borne yourself in the new government, and in the demonstration you have so freely given of your powers, you have added to that love we bear you, so much as to make it an infinite increase. Therefore congratulate the Magnificent Piero on having so worthy a son; congratulate also the people of Florence, in having so notable a defender of its liberties; and no less congratulate us, who have found a friend whose qualities will become greater with each day over the coming years. Perhaps it behoves us to exhort you to praiseworthy deeds, but your generous nature, so prone to worthy things, has no need of exhortation.

At that time, it was not thought that politics was synonymous with power and should be pursued without reference to values, religion, thought, learning or art. Lorenzo, the dukes of Milan, the kings of Naples, Ippolita Sforza and her husband the Duke of Calabria, Federigo of Urbino and the Malatesta family of Rimini, all the great political figures of Italy, even Pope Paul II, persecutor of humanists though he was, thought of politics as the pursuit of means to a humanly worth-while end, not as an end in itself. And among these, Lorenzo shone as a man combining artistic powers, learning, shrewd leadership and charm to perfection. He was near in all but looks to that 'perfect man' of Plato about whom everyone was thinking and talking. It was little wonder that he was known as 'The Magnificent'. That was a title given to all those who served in the Signoria. Today only rectors of Italian univer-sities receive it. But when one said 'The Magnificent' in Florence, without specifying the name, everyone knew to whom it referred.

Florence at this time was a splendid city for the young, and for ordinary people. There were constant spectacles, every kind of carnival, combining sweetness with ribaldry. In Venice people wore masks and costumes in carnival time, hiding their class. In Florence there was no need for that. There were rich and poor, but citizenship conferred an equality which was not all political humbug. Everyone danced and sang together in the streets, and brilliant young men like Lorenzo and Giuliano were seen all the time, coming and going without panoply from their home in the Via Larga, and they were loved like brothers. Giuliano was fine-looking, and even more popular than Lorenzo. In the latter, the future ruler could be felt, a certain authority that established its own distance. In Giuliano, there was simply an ideal young man.

Piero allowed Lorenzo to put on a joust in 1468, when he was twenty. By implication it was to honour his arrival at man's estate. The Medici tradition of not participating in great public spectacles, except as fellow citizens, still cast its shadow, but now things were different. The official reason for Lorenzo's joust was to celebrate the beauty of his mistress, Lucrezia Donati, and secondarily his forthcoming marriage to a Roman heiress, Clarice Orsini, who was no beauty but would give him healthy children. The engagement had been arranged largely by his mother, who had gone to Rome to look at the girl and had judged her, while no beauty like so many Florentine women, robust and entirely lacking in

ABOVE A tournament scene from 1460, in pen and brown ink. The Florentines, being a commercial people, preferred to employ others to do their fighting for them, and their jousts were accordingly harmless. Lorenzo wrote after his first joust, 'Although not a vigorous warrior, nor a very hard hitter, I got the first prize.'

BELOW LEFT The bust of an unknown lady by Andrea Verrocchio (1435–88). Some believe it to be a portrait of Lucrezia Donati, Lorenzo's mistress.

BELOW RIGHT A portrait by the school of Domenico Ghirlandaio of Clarice Orsini, wife of Lorenzo the Magnificent. She bore Lorenzo ten children, but died before she was forty, in 1487.

degenerate characteristics. It was hoped that the family gout would loosen its grip on the Medici tree after an injection of new blood, and certainly until now its marriages had tended towards the inbred. Besides this, Clarice had cardinals, archbishops and military generals as her closest relatives. The Orsini palace in Rome bustled with *condottiere* nephews. The family also held fiefs and high offices in Naples. Above all, they owned a long line of fortresses along the high road leading south out of Florence. There was nothing like securing one's trade routes in church.

The people of Florence, on the other hand, found the idea unappetising. The Orsini were a noble Teutonic family with vast possessions all round Rome. Clarice's mother belonged to the powerful Bracciani. It was not really a match for a commercial family who had no dreams of dynastic glory. Besides, Clarice could not compare with a Florentine girl from almost any middle-class family. She stood above middle height, with a fair skin and a tinge of red in her hair. But her face was too round to be attractive, though she did have a delicate neck and a nice figure. She also had long, pretty hands. But she walked and talked with her head bent forward, which no Florentine girl even of a working family would ever be seen doing. She was not highly educated. She was no wit. As for artistic tastes, one could not say that hers were bad: she had none at all. She was pious in a plodding sort of way, and looked like finding Florentine society, with its free and risqué talk, rather unbearable.

It seemed quite in order to celebrate her imminent arrival in Florence with poems of praise for one of the city's most extravagantly graceful and refined creatures, Lucrezia Donati, who was also Lorenzo's mistress. Niccolò Ardinghelli was sent on a foreign mission as soon as he married this beautiful creature, because Lorenzo was in love with her. Lorenzo took part in the joust as one of the contending knights. Though he was a powerful and vigorous young man, he really saw little point in driving a long spear into someone else, even with the point blunted. He wrote afterwards, 'Although not a vigorous warrior, nor a very hard hitter, I got the first prize, a helmet inlaid with silver and a figure of Mars on the crest.' No one begrudged him the bespoke prize. He looked his title of Magnificent, in a red and white surcoat and a scarf bearing the legend 'Le Tems Revient' embroidered with roses, some full-blown and others withered. Rubies, diamonds and pearls were sewn into his black velvet cap, which was pierced with a feather of gold thread spangled with more precious stones. The King of Naples had sent presents of horses and armour. So had the Dukes of Ferrara and Milan.

At the tournament, Lucrezia gave Lorenzo a wreath of violets. There was a diamond in his shield. For the combat, he put on another surcoat of velvet fringed with gold, its decoration the golden lilies of France (granted to the Medici by Louis XI) upon an azure ground, his helmet with three blue feathers instead of the former jewelled cap. It must have

been the gentlest joust ever staged. His horse was draped with pearl-
embroidered velvet in chequered red and white. Behind him in procession were trumpeters and drummers and fife-players, ten youths on
horseback and then, bringing up the rear, sixty-four foot soldiers in
armour.

About ten thousand ducats of good Medici money were spent on it.
Cosimo would not perhaps have recoiled from the idea. Such a joust
would not have been fitting in his day. Indeed, there had been no son to
be the apple of the people's eye. That was why he had put so much attention into Lorenzo's education. With a sphere of influence extending to
the Mediterranean on one side and the Adriatic on the other, and a
financial finger in every European fire, and princely alliances, the old
hidden leadership, pulling strings from behind, was no longer enough.
Everyone outside Florence treated Lorenzo like a prince. Florence
wanted it like that, though she pretended not to see him as anything
more than a rich citizen. She needed to be able to pull him down if he
became unbearable.

The following May, Clarice was brought to Florence. Few people
had anything good to say about this first Medici marriage to a 'foreigner'.
Some predicted that the match would produce negative results in
Lorenzo's heir and first-born, and they were not far wrong. His son was
to marry an Orsini girl too, and neither of them was liked. But Lorenzo
and Clarice were married on 4 June. In the Via Larga house, a ballroom
was set up. Clarice's dress was white with gold brocade, her horse a gift
from the Neapolitan stables. After the ceremony, she and fifty of
Florence's younger leading women dined on the balcony overlooking
the garden, while Lucrezia, Lorenzo's mother, entertained the older
women inside. As for the younger men, they were in the ballroom, while
the older citizens sat round the square courtyard under the arches, from
which one today enters the museum. There were forty stewards of noble
birth. At that time, Donatello's David stood in the garden at the centre
of a fountain, which was ringed with tables on which the wine stood in
huge coolers. Celebrations went on for three days, and each day a
hundred guests were entertained either at Via Larga or in the house of
Carlo de' Medici, one of Lorenzo's uncles. There was no undue extravagance of eating or drinking. In Florence there never was. There were
roast and boiled meats, jellies, cakes, sweets, Malvoisie and red Italian
wines, but no more than a modest middle-class family would expect to
have on the table for visitors. As entertainment, troops of horsemen
charged each other in mock warfare in the square, and there was a mock
infantry assault. Most pleasure was found in the ballroom, which was
hung with fabulous Persian carpets. There was music and dancing: in
this particularly Lorenzo revelled, and, as always when a public celebration came up, he took a part in writing the songs. He designed, he composed, he rehearsed, he sang.

A medal of Clarice Orsini,
Lorenzo's wife, with an
allegorical emblem on the
back. Grave and dutiful,
Clarice tended to disapprove
of Florentine manners, which
were freer at that time than
those of her native Rome.

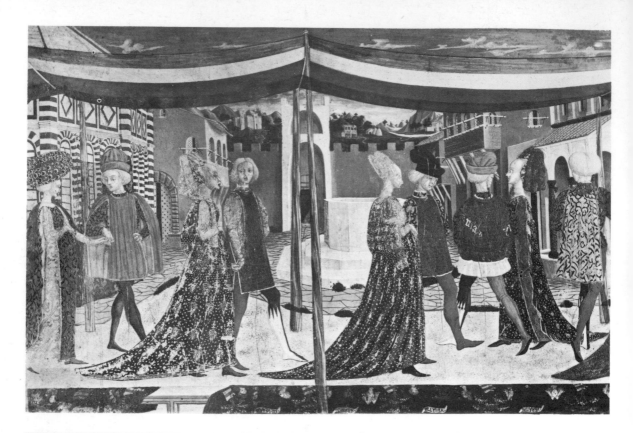

Details from the
Adimari chest.

LEFT The underside of a birth tray, the subject derived from Petrach's 'Triumph of Love'. In fifteenth-century Florence birth trays were used for bringing food to women in labour and were appropriately decorated.

BELOW Another Florentine birth tray showing the arms of the Samminiato and Gianfigliazzi families, who were joined in marriage, made between 1450 and 1475.

David commissioned by Cosimo de' Medici from Donatello for the Palazzo Medici in Florence.

When the party was over, he was sent on another diplomatic mission, this time back to Milan in the company of his tutor Gentile Becchi and his sister's husband. It was the journey of a prince, and intended as such in all but name. At Prato and Pistoia not far from Florence, he was received like one. He offended Lucca by staying the night outside the city walls, and had to delay his departure to make amends. He attended Mass, then made a speech to Lucca's Signoria which warmed and won their hearts. At Pietrasanta, he was dissuaded from putting up at the 'Bell Without the Walls' – the local inn – by the local Fieschi family who ruled the town for the Genoese commercial company of St George. He visited Sarzana just inland of La Spezia as he continued his way along the coast (writing poems on what he saw). Sarzana was already Medici property (purchased from Ludovico di Campo Fregoso together with the adjoining castle of Sarganella), as he intended to make Lucca and Pietrasanta Medici property too. The importance of Sarzana lay in the fact that it guarded the only road from the north along the coast: it could therefore check an invasion from the direction of Genoa, and neatly cut Lucca off from outside support.

The journey was slow not only because it was made on horseback but because there was much to do. Lorenzo's image had to stay. It was not won with power alone. His charm did as much as Medici money, in the sense that he made friends quickly. By his way of talking, he showed himself to be undevious and trustworthy. There is almost no known instance in his political life where he gave a promise and dishonoured it, or lied his way out of a corner: when he and Florence were in the tightest corner of its history, a decade later, he adopted the most open course he could think of, namely throwing himself on the mercy of the Neapolitan king and using his remarkable powers of personal persuasion. And it paid off. Only after his brother Giuliano was murdered did some shadowy events, such as the torturing of a pilgrim who called at one of his country houses and was taken for a conspirator, cloud his career.

He and Clarice wrote to each other frequently – affectionate and dutiful letters. He was well aware of the necessity of making a happy home, and with Clarice's stolid Roman co-operation he made one. There is no need to think that he was any more faithful than other husbands of the time. Love was always in his mind, and pretty women continued to make him happy or glum. In one of his songs, written like most of his other work with a poignant touch of irony which gives the lines their heart, he asked everyone – 'young girls and women, no matter who you are' – to take pity on him for the pain he was suffering:

Sempre servito io ho con pura fede
Una, la quale credea che fussi pietosa,
Et che dovessi haver di me merzede,
Et non, come era, fussi disdegnosa;
Hor m'ho perduto il tempo, et ogni cosa,
Che si rivolta, come al vento foglia.

LALVNA EPIANETA FEMININO POSTO NEPRIMO CIELO FREDA HE VMIDA ET FLEMATICHA M
EEANA TRALMONDO SVPERIORE ET LOINFERIORE AMA LAGEOMETRIA ET CIO CHEAESSA
ZA PARTIENE DIFACCIA TONDA DIZTRA MEEANA METALLI ALARGIENTO DELLE CHONP
MPLEZZIONI LAFREA DETENPI ELVERNO DEGLIELEMENTI LAQVA ELDI ZVO EILVENERDI CH
ONLAHORA PRIMA 8 15 E Z Z ELAZVA NOTTE EQVELLA DELVENERDI AMICO ZVO E GIOVE IN
IMICO MARTE A VNA ZOLA ABITAZIONE ELCHANCHRO PREZZO ASOLE EMETARCHVRIO LAEZAL
TAZIONE ZVA EILTAVRO LAMORTE OVERO VMILIAZIONE EZCORPIO VA IN 12 ZENGNI IN Z 8 DICOMICIANDO
DALCHANCHRO IN Z DI EL VA VNZENGNIO 15 GRADI PERDI Z ZMINVTI Z 6 ZECONDI PEDROPA EIN Z 8 DI ADIZCOR
ZI EZO IZ ZENGNI CHONPVZMENTE EPIV 8 GRADI E Z6 MINVTI E ZO ZECONDI E QVESTO ZIDIMOZRA
CHE PARTENDOZI LALVNA DAZOLE ETORNANDO AL   LOPAZZA PER 8 MINV TI E 14 ZECHONDI IN Z
DI E 13 ORE E QVESTO ZECONDO EMOVIMENTO DIMEEO

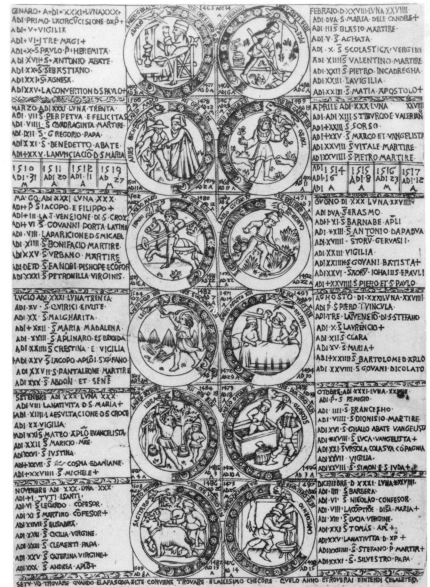

I have always served with pure fidelity one whom I thought kind, and who ought to have rewarded me and not proved unworthy, as she did. Now I have wasted my time and everything, and am turned over like a leaf in the wind!

The last stage of his journey was by Pontremoli to Milan. He became the godfather of the new Duke of Milan's child. Here too his personal fascination exercised itself on men and women alike. He gave the duchess a gold necklace and a large diamond worth 3,000 ducats. The duke wanted him as godfather for *all* his children, as who would not at that generous rate! Piero was not at all happy. Lorenzo had gone beyond his mandate and was forming personal alliances which might not fit in with Florentine requirements. The Milanese connection was no more popular than it had ever been. Galeazzo Maria, the young duke, had arrived in Florence during the recent war with no money in his pocket, and the city had had to fill it in order to get the war finished and trade roaring again. He was definitely not liked, and here was Lorenzo treating him like the king of France. Piero told his wife that 'he would not suffer that the goslings should lead the geese to drink'. And Lorenzo returned to Florence chastened, but all the more a diplomat for it.

His father died the following year, on 2 December 1469, at the age of fifty-three. Though Medici power was still not secure, he had cleverly introduced a certain aristocratic style without anyone noticing. Lorenzo was accepted as Florence's princely representative and leader, whether people liked it or not (or would stand for it or not). He had just as many powerful enemies as any other Medici before him but at least there would be no surprise at his 'succession' as there had been at Piero's.

All this Piero had managed from his sick-bed. He asked to be buried quietly, as he lived. Lorenzo and Giuliano commissioned a simple tomb from Verrocchio, which is still to be seen, gloomy and forbidding, in the cold style that was increasingly accepted as 'classical', in the old sacristy of San Lorenzo, the Medici church which Giovanni di Averardo had constructed out of its earlier twelfth-century form, though without destroying its sweetness. He too lies in the old sacristy. Piero and Lorenzo's uncle Giovanni were placed in the Verrocchio tomb together.

Like his grandfather and father before him, Piero left no will, only an inventory of his possessions and capital. Lorenzo found everything in order, to the value of 237,989 florins (about £10 million). He recorded this in a large green book on goatskin paper in his own hand, according to a brief history of his family which he himself wrote some years later. He also recorded that the Medici family had spent 'the incredible sum' of over half a million florins between 1434 and 1471 in charitable buildings and taxes alone.

OPPOSITE A Florentine calendar from 1464–65. It shows the saints' days, with drawings of various occupations and, above each drawing, a sign of the zodiac.

BELOW *Judith and Holofernes* by Donatello. Like the *David*, it was commissioned by Donatello's lifetime patron Cosimo de' Medici, for the Palazzo Medici in Florence.

Part Two

The Early Years of Lorenzo's Power, 1469-77

Now that he was no longer running diplomatic errands for his father, but head of the family, Lorenzo was not so sure that he would like to inherit the invisible, questionable and indeed forbidden throne his father had made for him. He wanted to stay as he was, a rich young man who had far more in him than wealth or political power could bestow. He wanted his friends, who dropped in casually and sat down at his dinner table without ceremony. He wanted his long hours of pleasure in the Mugello or Fiesole or Pisan hills, where he loved to hawk. He wanted his music and dancing. He wanted the conversations that stretched into the night, and seemed to achieve more in terms of civilisation than the cleverest power-politics. And he thought that he could stay as he was and keep the family as it was, the most influential in town and one of the most influential in Europe. Within a few hours of his father's death, he saw that this was not possible. The unacknowledged throne and the family wealth went together, and the loss of one meant the loss of the other.

In his brief memoir of his father's death, he wrote that

the chiefs of the city or the state came to our house to offer their condolences and to urge me to take over the affairs of the city or the state as my grandfather and my father did, which affairs, being unsuitable to my age, and heavy in responsibility, and dangerous, I accepted with reluctance, and only for the preservation of friends and patrimony, knowing how much we in Florence need the state.

The Medici party – which meant a number of notable families – depended on the Medici family, and an opposing party in power would soon have seen to it, by means of tax manipulation, that they counted for less. The party was far from strong at the moment, but Lorenzo could rely on support from abroad. One of his greatest admirers was Louis XI, who not long before had conferred the French lilies on the uppermost of the balls in the Medici arms. It was Lorenzo's judgment that he admired most.

Lorenzo accepted the succession the day after his father died. He had to govern to prevent others doing so. He never commanded an army in the field. At any time the executive could have trumped up charges against him. But he governed until his dying hour.

As it turned out, the threat to his power and person came from outside Florence. In the previous year, 1468, Paul II had tried hard to win Rimini. Sigismondo Malatesta, its ruler, died in October, a rather typical creature of his time in combining utter savagery where the senses were concerned

VIVE DVX ALEXANDER
MED SECVL A PER OMNIA

The Medici coat-of-arms in the Piazza Ognissanti, Florence. The *fleur de lys* was granted to Piero by Louis XI as a testimony of the traditional close friendship between France and Florence. During Lorenzo's life the number of armorial balls on the coat of arms was raised to six – five red and one blue.

with refinement in art and letters. The Pope claimed his town as a lapsed fief, since Malatesta had no legitimate issue. The bastard Ruberto Malatesta acted quickly and seized the lordship, and the triple alliance – Milan, Naples, Florence – supported him. So did Federigo of Urbino. The Pope's mercenary general, Alessandro Sforza, put Rimini to the siege but was defeated a few months before Piero died. Malatesta warned the Pope that he would call on the Turks for help if necessary, and since they were on the Albanian coast at the time, the Pope preferred to negotiate a peace. He would probably never get Rimini. Equally he would never forget Florence's role. That was to be the cause of Lorenzo's trouble, under a succeeding pope.

With an intelligence that everyone had come to expect in him, Lorenzo set about changing the constitution. There was to be a fresh scrutiny of the magistrates or *gonfalonieri* by the *Balìa*. Control of the lists would last five years. It regulated the council of one hundred by empowering forty to select fifty candidates drawn as magistrates, who would then, together with the forty, form an elective board for the hundred. To the outside world it looked gibberish, but the figures made sense inside Florence because they depended not on any logic but on the current state of Medici power. Had there been only thirty Medici supporters to select the magistrates, and only forty Medici-minded magistrate-nominees, the numbers would have read thirty and forty instead of forty and fifty. The idea was simply to alter the colour of the hundred. It was all done democratically, except that the constitution was rigged for the governing party.

The mass of the people took no part in all this not because there was less sense of freedom in the fifteenth century than there is now, but because pressure could not yet be exercised by numbers, unless there was a state of riot. There were not sufficient agglomerations at any level – of work, wealth or land ownership – to make pressure by numbers or votes necessary, much less possible. To improve one's lot, one tried to influence someone with whom one rubbed shoulders every day. The state was irrelevant to that operation: politics neither emerged from ordinary people nor led to them. When Lorenzo produced a more efficient governing machine, and this his constitutional changes certainly achieved, by giving the hundred a long term of five years and the power when necessary to act secretly and quickly as the executive power, more or less everyone was happy, because it produced a safer Florence too: which meant a city in which one might work peacefully and draw the expected reward. As for the poor devils out of work, and there were always a certain number, they were the objects of charity (as they still are). Only in times of acute unemployment, as during the period of the *ciompi* revolution, did their condition influence politics.

Lorenzo began to consult his party leaders separately, and then he followed his own course, thus treading the path of every wise prince who keeps his courtiers arguing with each other but never with him. He advanced new men and at the same time heaped honours on the old Medici-supporting families, by giving them embassies and offices – Antonio Pucci, Agnolo Niccolini, Piero Filippo Pandolfini, Bernardo del Nero, Bernardo Buongirolami among the younger men. He maintained that his father Piero ought to have done this, and that it would have prevented his government's failure in 1466.

Even in these first tender years, he took care to reconcile men who felt that they were being assessed too high tax-wise or that they deserved a job which they had not got – men like Guido Vespucci, Matteo Palmieri, Bartolomeo Valori, Luigi Guicciardini. Lorenzo was not by nature at all patient, but he forced himself to be. We have to remember that these men would write to him personally with their complaints, and that they blamed him and him alone if they failed to get the job or the tax rebate. The job or the rebate came to them from other sources, where his name was not mentioned, but his was the hand that invited the wheels to grind, however slowly they might do so.

He also took care to win back the junior line of his family which had latterly been kept at some distance. He realised that revolution sprang more easily from junior branches than from frankly opposed families. A number of cousins suddenly found themselves in the thick of financial or signorial affairs.

As he handed out largesse, he tightened state security. He gave fresh

A portrait of Galeazzo Maria Sforza, Duke of Milan, by Piero Pollainolo (1441–96). He visited Florence in 1471 and was murdered in 1476 in Milan Cathedral, bringing to an end two decades of peace among the Italian states.

powers to the Eight of Watch and Ward. The *Podestà* sank in importance but a *bargello di contado* (rural police-chief), with a mounted police force, kept order in the country, after a riot almost developed in Prato. He was firmly in the saddle.

He could now have his own way over Milan too. In March 1471 the Duke and Duchess of Milan rode into Florence with a train of two thousand horses and two hundred mules, the gold and silver cloth of their retinue glittering in the spring sunshine. It was an eight-day visit, and they lodged at the Via Larga house. Lorenzo and Giuliano were the leaders and devisers of the hectic fun. They enjoyed themselves and had the satisfaction of seeing the people won over to this military state in the north, at least for the length of the stay. The church of Santo Spirito caught fire during the performance of a sacred play called *The Descent of the Holy Ghost*. This put the popularity of the Milanese back a bit, as it was taken by the superstitious minds of the time (and all minds were superstitious) as a sign of divine wrath, especially as the guests had eaten meat during the Lenten season. The wise predicted that the city would one day pay for this.

Lorenzo threw himself into popular amusements with the same vigorous concentration as he did everything else. Even here he took a re-forming hand. He revived the old Maypole dances which he loved so much and which survived only in the country. He brought back the old country sports. He organised the saturnalia and turned the crude ribaldries of the processions and maskers into really amusing ones. That was no less a *'Renaissance'* than what went on in thought and art. It meant reviving ancient Roman customs, which were still alive in the people. In the same way, he did everything to keep alive the language the people talked, which was why Luigi Pulci, the writer of the taverns, could command so much of his heart and time. They often worked together on the cars for a carnival procession, devising scenes – an old man cuckolded by a young wife was a favourite one. Under Lorenzo the carnival became something to delight the ear and eye. He composed many of the carnival songs himself:

> *Quant'è bella giovinezza,*
> *che si fugge tuttavia!*
> *Chi vuol esser lieto, sia;*
> *di doman non c'e certezza.*

How marvellous youth is – but it's gone in a moment! Whoever wants to be happy, let him be so, there's nothing certain in tomorrow.

> *Donne e giovinetti amanti,*
> *viva Bacco e viva Amore!*
> *Ciascun suoni, balli e canti!*
> *Arda di dolcezza il core!*
> *Non fatica, non dolore!*

A marriage chest or *cassone* showing a tournament scene.

Cio c'ha a esser, convien sia.
Chi vuol esser lieto, sia:
di doman non c'e certezza.

Women and young lovers, long live Bacchus and long live Love! Let everyone play and sing and dance, let the heart burn with sweetness, no work, no pain! It's better to be as you want to be. So whoever wants to be happy, let him! There's nothing certain in tomorrow!

Lorenzo loved Florence. In the city's carnivals there were always bands of men dressed as women and girls, parading the streets and singing bawdy songs. Mostly, these songs were boring and tasteless until Lorenzo came along. He devised carnival cars with classical themes – Bacchus and Ariadne, or the powers of nature. Behind the cars would come hundreds of the smartest Florentine youths on foot or horseback, playing instruments. On May Day, girls would dance round the Maypole to Poliziano's ballads. It was perhaps the classical element that distressed Savonarola more than the licence. In his attitudes there was both the fierce desire to reform the Church of its luxury and indulgence, like the German reformers of the next century, and an equally fierce reaction to this very reform, in a stricter orthodoxy than ever before. When Savonarola was in power, and Lorenzo dead, the carnivals went on, but Heinrich Isaak's music accompanied not Lorenzo's sweet and harmless songs but hymns. The Church as a whole was never sympathetic to Lorenzo, and this may account for the fact that his name

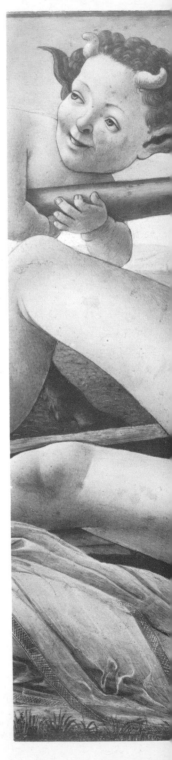

A stone plaque on the façade of a house in Florence forbidding prostitutes to live in the Santa Croce area. This was part of a plan not to root out prostitution but to keep certain areas 'clean'.

was swallowed in oblivion soon after his death, so effectively that even today many educated people have barely heard his name.

Nor was this due to his liking pretty women. His grandfather Cosimo had liked them too, and given at least one of them a child without marrying her. That was too much common practice for the Church to disapprove. Popes had a way of producing 'nephews' who looked remarkably like themselves. Fornication was not thought anti-Christian. The gayer the young man, the healthier he was considered. Lorenzo was not a silent and reflective man like his grandfather Cosimo. But like many people who are versatile without being dilletante, he was overwrought. Life had so many objectives for him that time seemed too short. The deepest objective of them all – the search for God – was the most elusive:

> *O Dio, O Sommo bene, or come fai?*
> *Che te sol cerco e non truovo mai?*

Oh God, oh height of goodness, now what will you do – that I seek you alone and can never find you?

His carnival songs were never crude. They were, if anything, pedantic, heavy with literary allusion, compared with what had been sung in the streets before. But they were all the more erotic for that. He wrote a series designed to be sung by maskers in the clothes of various crafts. There was 'the song of the perfumes', 'the song of the wafer biscuits', 'the song of the tree-grafters'. They are all addressed to women, and the feminine audiences of Florence were excited and provoked by what they heard, and by the accompanying gestures. The perfumier's song tells the women 'We are young gallants from Valencia who happen to be passing'. But they are already bound to Florence by love for the city's women. There are nice, pretty women in their own country too, but Florentine women beat them every time. Now 'if you're not in love, it's no use being beautiful'. As to their trade, 'We have bottles as long as

A detail from Botticelli's *Venus and Mars*. Venus as love and concord is opposed to Mars, symbol of hate and discord. She conquers him by reason of the harmony of opposites, according to Ficino and Pico della Mirandola.

your hand' (these were the long-necked phials used for perfume). If the women did not believe it, they could have them in their hands to feel. Little by little a delightful smell would 'spill out', right at the centre of that little fire.

And we would also like to mention our oil. It also has a nice smell, and a lot of strength. It does your body good from top to bottom. It comes out drop by drop. The more slowly it comes out, the more potent it is. Oil dulls every pain, soothes all your troubles. It draws the heat. The harder you rub the more its sweetness penetrates. If you have the shivers or a fever, try our oil and you'll get better.

And they had a good soap too. It makes a nice lather. Rub a piece wherever you want it. Again, the more you rub, the more comes. 'Has it never happened to you, ladies, that your ring was too tight? Rub a bit of soap on, and it'll get bigger. . . . Ladies, whatever we have is yours! If you are alight with love, put some of our oil on, grease yourself at our expense!'

'The song of the wafer biscuits' tells the women 'We are young, and past masters at making biscuits. These are so good that we had to be chased out of the shop: we were eating them as fast as we made them!' But without women, things were no good. So, 'We'll teach you how to do it'. You put some water in a bowl and as much flour as you can get in. Then you mix it, until it gets like a watery paste, rather like macaroni water. 'If you don't want to get too tired use your right hand and not your left. Throw some nice white sugar in, but don't on any account stop kneading. And be careful that none spills over.' Once the dough is ready, you taste it with your finger. If it's good you put the moulds on the fire to get ready. Heat them well. If they are new forms, heat them slowly, and grease them carefully. If they are old and used you can put in as much dough as you like. The ladles from Bologna are good for that kind of job. When the dough is in and beginning to cook, you hold the irons tight, shift the forms around, turn them upside down, until they're done. The dough often spills over, but this is all right. When it's cooked enough, open the forms and take out the biscuit. If it has been well greased, it'll come out easily. Then fold it and put it in a white cloth. Take a brush and a rough cloth and clean the forms well. They're rather like a pike's mouth, dough gets in the creases. If you'd like your biscuit bigger, that's all right. Or you can have two at the same time – one you hold, the other you slip in (to your mouth), and it's very nice. If they're nicely cooked and red, they're the best, and you can eat as many as you like. If they come out good and big, squeeze them a bit and take small bites. 'Ladies, hold the moulds and we'll put them in. If we put them in too hard or too soft, take hold of the ladle yourself and put them in yourself, because they're really good.'

'The song of the tree-grafters' begins, 'Ladies, we're masters of grafting. We know how to do it, any way you like. And if you'd like to learn how, we'll teach you little by little. You don't need to study it up – everyone knows how to do something natural.' The tree you are grafting has to be young, tender, long, without knots and healthy. Its bark should be nice and clean and delicate, when it starts to move and shoot (that is, put out shoots). Make a little opening half way down the other tree, as narrow as you can, in case the bark breaks ('bursts'). Push the graft in as hard as you can, then tie it round with a willow branch and allow for the two to mix together well. With your hand, softly open the fissure, again without tearing, and then push (*ficca*, from *ficcare* 'to thrust', but *fica* also means the female organ) the stem in. If it rains, cover it up and leave it a few days. Whoever wants good oil must graft the olive tree. The drill is the same. And you get nice big apples and figs this way too. Just make the opening, and then slip it in. Do it with care. You'll ruin everything if you go too fast. Better to wait for the right season, when the tree is sweet and on the suck. The tree that is at first rough and wild can bit by bit be made nice and soft with grafting. Ladies, we invite you to graft everything, if it doesn't rain and stays dry!'

This was the kind of thing that made Savonarola itch for a box of matches. He quite rightly saw it as connected in some way with so-called pagan thought, and current classical aspirations. Though not lacking in ancient learning himself, he cried at Florence's humanists, 'An old woman knows more about faith than your Plato!' He scorned Botticelli's naked Venus.

Botticelli's *Birth of Venus*, commissioned by Lorenzo di Pierfrancesco de' Medici, Lorenzo's second cousin.

Neither Lorenzo nor Botticelli scorned him in return. They listened and they thought hard. Botticelli became one of Savonarola's most ardent followers, like so many of Lorenzo's closest friends, including the architect whom Lorenzo nicknamed '*Il Cronaca*' (the chronicle) because he never entered his studio without a new story about the beloved Savonarola. Nor did Lorenzo himself put a brake on the castigating priest. Only once or twice did he pass a message to him through friends that he should curb his denunciations of the city's leading families. Savonarola took no notice, and Lorenzo took no action. At any time, he could have stopped Savonarola's career in mid-stream. As it was, Savonarola became prior of St Mark's without his intervention, and began building up the support which later overturned Medici rule.

There was a reason for his success. His sermons echoed something everyone felt, and which Lorenzo felt perhaps more deeply than most: that in earlier times people had been simpler and sounder, and this soundness had come from their faith. While he worked for the new civilisation, and longed for the 'release that Plato and Christ promised', Lorenzo was conscious of some warmth having departed. We can read this uncertainty in his verse, as if money had failed to buy the right luxury, the spiritual sort. It is little wonder that Savonarola found such rapt audiences, and as much among the rich as the poor. He pointed to a world in which the power and luxury were gone, but which was gayer for all that. This is why his voice seems to echo in Lorenzo's *laudi* and spiritual poems:

> *Muoia in me questa mia misera vita,*
> *accio che viva, o vera vita, in te;*
> *la morte in multitudine infinita,*
> *in te sol vita sia, che vita se';*
> *muoio, quando te lascio e guardo me;*
> *converso a te, io non morro giamai.*

This my poor life dies in me so that it may live, oh true life, in you! Death in its infinite multitudes can only have life in you, because you are life itself. I die when I look to myself, but talking to you I never die again.

In 1470 a group of Florentines exiled by Piero back in 1466, and led by Bernardo Nardi, rushed the town of Prato with the purpose of using it as a springboard for an attack on Florence, and imprisoned the *Podestà*. However, a young knight of Rhodes called Giorgio Ginori, who happened to be there, collected a group of volunteers and surrounded the rebels, then released the *Podestà*.

A successful riot in a subject town not thirty miles from Florence might have set Pope Paul II's mind working. As luck had it, he died and was succeeded by Francesco della Rovere, who knew much more about theology than Paul but was no less irascible. He was also unpopular in Rome. But he and Lorenzo got on when the latter was chosen by the

Signoria to head an embassy of congratulation in Rome, and to attend the coronation. At the Vatican, Lorenzo was 'much honoured', as he himself wrote, and the Pope gave him two marble heads, one of Augustus and the other of Agrippa, which he brought back to Florence together with cameos and medallions. He probably asked the Pope for a cardinal's hat for his brother Giuliano, hoping that he would one day be pope. He got no definite assurances, but at least it looked as if the rift with Rome had been healed.

Soon after he got back, another subject town rebelled. This was Volterra. Its town council had quarrelled with the Florentine company which had a lease on an alum mine in the Maremma without proper legal right. The council occupied the pit, and the company appealed to Florence, since Florentine shareholders were behind it. Lorenzo at first

A portrait in marble bas relief of Federigo da Montefeltro, Duke of Urbino, by Gian Cristofero Romano (c. 1470–1512). He patronised the Florentine bookseller Vespasiano da Bisticci and many artists including Piero della Francesca and Pisanello. A military leader, Federigo was a sometime ally of Lorenzo's.

showed caution, withdrawing some of the more headstrong members of the company to Florence. But he upheld the company's right to have the mine. A popular riot in Volterra was the result. Two of the shareholders were murdered. The local Signoria protected the Florentine *Podestà* from them, with difficulty, and did its best to cool tempers on both sides.

Lorenzo took the hard line, prompted by political rather than commercial motives, since the mine in question was poor and never used again. Tommaso Soderini argued for peace, which probably provoked Lorenzo to decide on war. He knew that he had the people behind him, and he needed to be seen as strong. He doubled the committee known as the Ten of War. He borrowed one hundred thousand florins from the state fund for dowries. He asked Federigo of Urbino to command an army of 5,500 men, with contingents from the Pope and the Duke of Milan. He got some slight help too from Siena and Piombino. The army advanced across the lovely Elsa valley, and attacked Volterra from the south. Its artillery smashed the walls, and Volterra's mercenaries refused to fight.

After a twenty-five day siege, the city capitulated. A general sack followed after a scuffle between a Venetian mercenary and one of the local soldiers. The generals were unable to restrain their troops. It was a horrible accident, and one that Lorenzo never forgot. Houses were ransacked and rased, and the women raped. The moment he heard the news, he hurried to Volterra himself and distributed relief, reassuring the citizens that they would not be troubled again (if they remained faithful Florentines). Subsequently he spent great sums of money on estates which he bought in the area. He learned what a tough political programme looked like when it came down to the human beings.

But it was a triumph for him. The Pope gave him the sole lease of his alum mines near Civitavecchia. He had already, during Lorenzo's visit to Rome, formally invested the Medici bank as treasurer of the papal funds. Giovanni Tornabuoni, Medici bank-manager in Rome, was allowed to purchase many of the fabulous jewels collected by the late Paul II. It looked as if Florence could do no wrong at the Vatican.

In return for this service at Volterra, Lorenzo gave to Federigo of Urbino one of the unoccupied Pitti villas as well as Florentine citizenship. He crowned him with a helmet of silver. On the crest of a hill to the south of Volterra, he built a huge castle which still mars the city's appearance today. Volterra's mineral rights – in salt, sulphur, alum and copper – were now vested in Florence.

Lorenzo's harsh reaction to the riot, which the Signoria of Volterra could probably have dealt with on its own, no doubt had something to do with the shaky financial condition of the Medici company. It had reached its maximum expansion under Cosimo. The rest of its career was to be one of decline. But the most that could be said at this time was that the Medici branches were not doing as well as they might be. No one seemed to know why. Today a firm at that point of development would become involved in a big expansion programme, a take-over or a partnership with another group. That did not happen. Other men north of the Alps were building firms equally strong. The future was to lie with groups like the Fugger brothers of Augsburg, who financed Charles v in his election as Holy Roman Emperor in the following century, and had powerful investments in every part of Europe.

Lorenzo was as little a business man as his father had been. Bad financial policies over the next twenty years made matters worse. Neither he nor Piero before him had Cosimo's gift of choosing the right branch-manager, or of overseeing him properly. In 1472 the London bank was

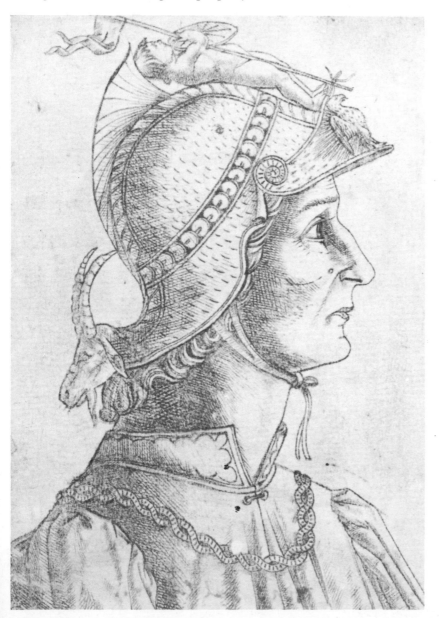

A fantastic helmet, made around 1470, most probably for one of Florence's jousts. Lorenzo's prize at his first joust in 1468 was a helmet inlaid with silver, a figure of Mars on the crest.

1920—2—14—1 (7)

closed down, owing to its failure to recoup on Edward IV's debt. It was put under the jurisdiction of the Bruges branch, though the following year a Medici office was again opened in London owing to the enormous importance of English wool to the Florentine market. That year too there was a series of difficulties at Bruges, due partly to its inheriting the London debt, partly to its own failure to get back the moneys it had loaned to Charles the Bold of Burgundy. When Charles the Bold died in 1477, he left a debt with the bank of about £9,000, at least according to the branch-manager, Portinari. Lorenzo found the figure very wide of the mark. He thought it was more in the region of £16,000. There had been additional lendings to Mary of Burgundy, Charles's daughter, and to her husband Maximilian of Austria. Portinari was in the habit of lending in order to advance his own interests rather than Medici ones. He mixed with people whom he considered more powerful than Lorenzo. Herein lay the chief source of Florence's difficulties. It was being outpaced by the world north of the Alps. Italian states were simply not big enough to cope with the northern agglomerations, which fact led to the downfall of every one of them sooner or later. In the end even the great Venice dwindled into an interesting town.

Lorenzo was shrewd enough but found himself obliged to leave things to men he could not trust. Portinari was in the habit of taking about 45% of the profits on any wool transaction by the Medici bank: his legal share was $27\frac{1}{2}\%$. He was also liable for losses to this amount, but here he was careful to go by the legal equity, thus neatly transferring losses to Lorenzo. At first the latter failed to see what was going on. He eventually decided to discontinue his association with the Portinari brothers, who had caused him a vast loss while becoming rich and powerful men themselves. The Bruges bank too was liquidated in 1481.

Thus we should not be surprised that the Medici régime crashed so quickly after Lorenzo's death, despite his popularity and the apparent success of his government. Economic depression (not only in the case of the Medici business, either) was the fact underneath the glamour. It accounted for his nervous neutrality towards the end of his life. The Medici, while being masters of money, had little sense of investment. They went in for lending – to princes who squandered the money on their courts or their wars, and to *condottieri* inside Italy who did not always win. There was also throughout the fifteenth century a marked lack of investment possibility. But a deliberate programme of investment might have saved the Medici interests, and particularly some form of partnership with a rich, up-and-coming man north of the Alps. By the natural evolution of events, the Medici fortune gradually became smaller by remaining static. Few people understood that a new society had come about in which turbulence seemed to be the basic condition. It was in a continual state of expansion, which left no business safe for more than a few decades.

The left panel from an altarpiece commissioned by the
Portinari family from the
Flemish painter Hugo van der
Goes. It shows St Matthew and
St Antony recommending the
banker Tommaso Portinari
(kneeling) and his two sons.
Portinari was the manager of
the Medici bank in Bruges. He
lived like a prince and often
seemed more interested in
advancing his own
connections with royalty than
in the Medici fortunes.

OPPOSITE The right panel of
the Portinari altarpiece,
designed for S. Egidio in
Florence, shows Mary
Magdalene and St Margaret
recommending Portinari's
wife and daughter, who are
kneeling.

Lorenzo's Policy of Expansion

In 1472 Lorenzo revived the decayed university of Pisa by making it a branch of Florence University, after coming to the conclusion that Florence was too distracting for students anyway, and lacked sufficient lodging space. By now, Florence had some kind of official university system, or at least a few professors. He also made use of the new situation for partly political ends.

Pisa hated her subjection to Florence more than any other Tuscan city. She had once been on the level of Genoa and Venice as a maritime republic. She had virtually owned Sardinia, together with the Genoese. Her fleet had fought with Venice's in a Crusade and then had fallen out with her about who should own what. After her defeat by Genoese ships in 1284, her decline had set in. She never forgot her days of glory, and resented Florence all the more warmly for it. Lorenzo decided to do something about it. On the whole he succeeded, though even today Florence is still something of a dirty word there.

Also Pisa was a dull place, and full of empty houses. It was malarial. Lorenzo decided to move all the faculties except philosophy and philology to Pisa, subsidising it out of Florentine and papal funds, as well as a handsome private endowment of his own. Both branches of this one university were to be regulated by a board of five, of which he was a founder member. He felt that if Pisa could not have the greater number of students, at least she should get the best professors. This is why Pisa University became prominent for law, medicine and theology, its basic subjects of that time, while remaining something of a backwater as a town. Malaria often drove the students away, but Lorenzo had draining operations started, and planted grass everywhere.

Also the new university showed (in a kindly way) that Florence was now lord of all Tuscany. Lorenzo had huge estates in the immediate neighbourhood. The university became popular with young Roman ecclesiastics, and his son Giovanni, later Pope Leo X, was a student there. So were Cesare Borgia, Alessandro Farnese and Pope Paul III.

His high reputation abroad kept him safe for the time being. England needed him for favours. So did the royal House of Aragon in Spain. In 1473 Louis XI commissioned him to arrange a marriage between the Dauphin and a Neapolitan princess, though King Ferrante, in his letter of reply to Lorenzo, pointed out that he did not wish to become the enemy of either the Duke of Burgundy or the Spaniards, as Louis XI seemed to require. The marriage did not take place. But then Louis XI probably only wanted to delay the already planned marriage between

Ferrante's daughter and the Duke of Savoy, which he knew about. As it was, the Dauphin married the Duke of Brittany's daughter, and later became Charles VIII: he incidentally evicted Ferrante's successors from Naples too. But however Lorenzo might draw a blank in some of his negotiations, he remained the most trusted ruler in Italy, if not in Europe. One could rely on his advice and – what was much more remarkable – his word.

Lorenzo seemed surrounded by well-wishers (a condition that in politics invariably hides dangers). The death of Paul II seemed to have healed his rifts with Rome for all time, as well as those between Rome and Naples. He did not join the Pope's holy league against the Turks after their capture of Negroponte from Venice. That would have offended Milan irreparably. But he made the friendliest anti-infidel noises.

Milanese tactics were clearly to embroil Lorenzo with other states, and he fell into the Duke of Milan's trap, in the form of a cool suggestion that he should try to seize Piombino, a port in southern Tuscany, while the going was good. Piombino was too good a plum for Lorenzo to miss,

A lunette by Giorgio Vasari (1511–71) from the Palazzo Vecchio in Florence, showing Lorenzo surrounded by philosophers and writers. When the Medici returned as dukes of Florence in the sixteenth century, they commissioned works glorifying their earlier, republican, past.

what with the Pope, Milan and Venice on his side. He thought the risk well-worthwhile. Lorenzo's plot, engineered by Piombinan exiles at Pistoia, was discovered, however, and King Ferrante of Naples snarled nastily at him, as Piombino was in the hands of the Appiani family under his protection, but the dust settled quickly afterwards.

His brother Giuliano was sent to Milan to return the eight-day visit of the Duke and Duchess. Then he went on to Venice, where he was fêted like a prince. Medici diplomacy and money were much needed at this time to cover Lorenzo's tentative expansionist policy (designed in turn to balance the bad state of trade). He had no sooner got his fingers burned at Piombino than he jumped into the fire again at Imola. This town lay on the road between Rimini and Bologna, a most attractive place to own, from Florence's point of view, because it would put her commodities within easy reach of the Adriatic coast and draw her closer to her commercial clients, the Manfredi of Faenza. It would also open a pass across the Apennines. Formerly Imola had belonged to the Manfredi but it was now for sale, chiefly under Milan's wing. Sixtus IV wanted it, as the basis of a state for one of his nephews, but the Duke of Milan had promised it to Lorenzo. The Pope then persuaded the Duke to go back on his word (not a difficult thing to accomplish), in exchange for the marriage of the Duke's illegitimate daughter Caterina to Girolamo Riario, the papal nephew whom Sixtus wanted to see installed in the Romagna with Imola as his base. With the bridegroom would come the sum of 40,000 ducats. Despite all Lorenzo's efforts, the deal went through.

It soon became clear that Girolamo Riario was out to establish a state of his own on Medici borders. He was after Faenza and Forlì too. Meanwhile, the Pope was having trouble at Spoleto, Todi, Città di Castello and other towns in Umbria. Niccolò Vitelli (a member of one of Città di Castello's leading families and as brutal a man as Girolamo) had taken over his own city and was defying papal troops. As a precaution against a papal retaliation, Lorenzo massed troops at Borgo San Sepolcro, about twelve miles from Città di Castello, to the north. This did the Pope's liver no good at all, seeing that San Sepolcro was only on lease to Lorenzo from the previous Pope. It looked as if everyone was going to have a fight. This did not happen because no one was sure who was his friend and who his enemy. It would take time for the new *status quo* to make itself clear. Meanwhile, Venice smoothed everything over with the Pope, and Lorenzo and Sixtus were soon smiling at each other again.

There was something sour in the smile, however, especially when the Archbishop of Florence, Pietro Riario, died and Sixtus wanted Francesco Salviati, another favourite, to take over the vacant archbishopric. Lorenzo opposed him, and the Pope saw that there was nothing to be done. He agreed that the see should go to Clarice's brother, Rinaldo Orsini, while Salviati (seething with anger) got Pisa when it fell vacant. Even this Florence opposed, and when Salviati was ready to possess his

A detail from Benozzo Gozzoli's fresco *The Journey of the Magi*. It shows, from left to right, Piero, Cosimo and the Duke Salviati.

own see, Lorenzo stopped him entering the city. In September 1474 Florence, Milan and Venice entered an *entente* together, which Rome and Naples might also enter if they wished. It sent the Pope into closer relations with Naples, and Ferrante visited Rome the following year for the signature of a formal alliance.

Still, Lorenzo had not quarrelled with either of them. No one seemed to want war. The recent brush over Imola looked like a harmless scuffle between friends. The Italian sky looked serene and clear, and a mellow peacefulness settled over the peninsula such as it had never known before in Christian times. A Ferrarese envoy wrote that peace was spreading so fast throughout Italy that 'unless the impossible occurs there will be more to say about the battles between birds and dogs, than about those between men'.

The house-warming of the Medici régime came with Giuliano's tournament in 1475, again in the Piazza Santa Croce. Officially, it was to celebrate the new friendship with Venice and the Pope, but in fact to honour Giuliano's mistress Simonetta, wife of Marco Vespucci, a much-loved woman in Florence. Giuliano wore silver armour wrought by Verrocchio, and bore a standard painted by Botticelli, representing Simonetta as Pallas Athene in a flowery meadow. Apart from openly glorifying the Medici brothers and continuing Piero's policy of creating a medieval and knightly atmosphere round the city's most commercial family, the joust helped to lay the memory of a severe famine three years before, the effects of which were still vivid in people's minds.

Then something happened which in a moment turned Italy from the land of peace into the land of war. The Duke of Milan was murdered. He was only thirty-two. It happened on 26 December 1476, as he entered

SIMONETTA IANVENSIS VESPVCCIA

San Stefano. He was stabbed to death by three Milanese noblemen and their bravos. The ambassadors present grasped hold of the Duke as he staggered forward, thinking that he had fainted, so quick were the murderers. Every Court in Europe was shocked by the news. The Milanese noblemen involved were Lampugnani, who had been condemned to death by Francesco Sforza and pardoned by his son; Visconti, who was avenging an insult to his sister; and Olgiati, who was a republican idealist. The thing was instigated by a certain Cola Montano, a teacher of rhetoric. They rehearsed every detail many times in a quiet sidestreet behind the church of Sant' Ambrogio. They improvised every conceivable movement the Duke could make. Lampugnani struck the first blow. He broke through the crowd and knelt before the Duke on the pretext of presenting a petition, then drove a knife into his belly. The others fell on the stricken man, and dozens more blows finished him off. Everyone escaped except Lampugnani, who slipped on a woman's train. He was hanged, together with his bravos. A few days later, the others were found. Olgiati fainted when he heard the bloodthirsty crowd as they crossed the city, dragging Lampugnani's mutilated body with them. When the news reached Rome, Sixtus IV said, 'The peace of Italy is dead.'

The Duke's widow, Bona of Savoy, assumed the regency for her infant son. Lorenzo at once despatched two of his most active diplomats, Luigi Guicciardini and Tommaso Soderini to support her. A revolt in Genoa against Milan was crushed. But more trouble came from the Duke's restless brothers, who returned to Milan. The Duke's widow was forced to exile them. Milan was not a strong state any more, and the three exiles could breed disturbances in Rome and Naples. Ruberto San Severino, their chief instigator, had a large estate near Naples. When a state like Milan was going for the most ruthless bidder, peace could not last much longer.

It was becoming clear, too, that Sixtus was seeing Lorenzo with new eyes. Florence financed certain rebel lords of the Romagna. She supported Carlo Fortebraccio, the *condottiere*, who was anxious to recover his family's position of leadership in Perugia. Lorenzo dissuaded him from this but Fortebraccio raided the countryside round Siena. Again Lorenzo induced him to withdraw, but it brought papal and Neapolitan troops into the field. The Pope alone was harmless enough, but joined to Naples he might well destroy Florence, now that Milan was no longer the strong man at her back door. Ferrante of Naples did not like Lorenzo's friendship with Venice. His envoy at Florence argued that while Cosimo had always struggled to curb Venetian ambitions, Lorenzo was encouraging them. It was clear that whereas even a year before it had been difficult to start a war, now it was impossible to keep the peace. Suddenly Lorenzo was everyone's enemy, and it was decided to get rid of him.

OPPOSITE A portrait of the lovely Simonetta Vespucci, wife of Marco Vespucci and mistress of Giuliano de' Medici, painted by Piero di Cosimo (1462–1515). In 1475 a famous joust, celebrated in verse by Agnolo Poliziano, was staged officially to mark Florence's new alliance with the Pope and Venice but in fact to celebrate her beauty.

Part Three

The Pazzi Conspiracy and the Crisis of Lorenzo's Career

The Pazzi chapel, designed around 1430 by Filippo Brunelleschi. Attached to the church of Santa Croce, the chapel is one of the finest and most classical buildings of the early Renaissance.

Ever since the Medici had entered politics, it had been necessary for them to watch rival families in case they became too powerful: if you tried to hold them back, they became envious; if you showered offices and embassies on them, they became rivals. The Pazzi were a noble House which had entered public life with great success, and become one of the richest groups in the city. Piero de' Pazzi had been one of the most popular men in Florentine history. Returning from an embassy in France, he hung behind his retinue so that he would be acclaimed by the people on entering the city. They not only acclaimed him but knighted him. The Pazzi had commercial enterprises everywhere in Europe, and like the Medici they were international bankers.

In Florence, however, they were never quite popular as a family, despite Piero de' Pazzi, mainly because they showed excessive pride. Unlike the Medici, they lacked the amiable gift of equality. In a letter to

The interior of the Pazzi chapel, classical and geometrical in its plan and use of contrasting colours.

her son, dated March 1462 (the year Piero de' Pazzi got his knighthood), Alessandra Strozzi wrote, 'I must remind you that those who are on the side of the Medici have always done well, and those on the side of the Pazzi the contrary – so be careful.' But then the son of Piero de' Pazzi married Lorenzo's favourite sister, Bianca, so it looked as if the families had merged. That was not the case.

Alone, the Pazzi family would have done nothing. But Lorenzo had angered the Pope. It was not only that he had wanted to buy Imola, he had tried to stop the Pope buying it. Lorenzo had asked Francesco de' Pazzi, head of the Pazzi bank in Rome, and one of thirty-two rival bankers in that city, not to advance Sixtus IV any sums of money for its purchase. He thought he could rely on Pazzi as a near-relative and a fellow-Florentine. He was mistaken. Pazzi went straight to the Pope and told him what Lorenzo had suggested. He then advanced Sixtus three-quarters of the money he needed. After that, Francesco de' Pazzi could do no wrong at the Vatican. Girolamo Riario, the Pope's nephew, seemed to live for him. And the Pazzi were clearly, from the papal point of view, better people to run Florence than the Medici. The Pope transferred his account from the Medici bank to the Pazzi.

A plot of some sort would anyway have resulted, but what Lorenzo now did made it certain. He had a law passed retrospectively that in the case of a Florentine dying intestate, the preference was to be given to collateral males over the daughter of the deceased. Thus the rich inheritance from Giovanni Borromeo would pass not to his daughter (incidentally the wife of Giovanni de' Pazzi) but to his own nephews. It was revenge pure and simple. Even Giuliano de' Medici saw that it was the rash act of a young man, stung by Francesco de' Pazzi's duplicity, and said so. Such a flagrant use of the state for private purposes did not look well. So a plot was hatched in Rome, sooner than it might otherwise have been.

It was the work of Girolamo Riario and Francesco de' Pazzi. The latter was a bachelor (a mistrusted category in Italy to this day, unless he is safe inside a monastery), and precisely the kind of man who got himself and those nearest him into disastrous trouble. He was a small man, full of a restless and interfering energy which craved an outlet. He dressed with great care, and puffed himself up in company. He was envious. Above all, he had more passion than mind, and a thought had only to pass through his head for it to seem a sacred trust. From the start, the plot seemed a sure-fire thing.

The Archbishop of Pisa, still seething at Lorenzo, was only too happy to join in. The three decided to hire a mercenary captain called Gian Battista da Montesecco to do the killing. There would be an army waiting outside Florence to occupy it. Niccolò da Tolentino, a more famous mercenary, was to approach the city from the east with his army, while a citizen of Città di Castello, Lorenzo Giustini, who could not forgive Lorenzo de' Medici for supporting the Vitelli family in his city (though his support was not proven), would lead an army northwards from Città di Castello. The Pope was kept informed. He adamantly refused to countenance the shedding of blood, and even called his nephew a scoundrel for hinting at such an idea. Whether this was only official tenderness, no one can tell. It remains that no plot of this kind can succeed without the shedding of blood, and the blood of the government too. Sixtus IV had every interest in removing Lorenzo, and to judge by his fits of rage later, whenever Lorenzo was mentioned, he was after his blood no less than Girolamo.

The rest of Francesco de' Pazzi's family were not so easy to convince. Renato protested against it and urged that time would get rid of the Medici anyway, since Lorenzo's financial affairs were in such a mess. Renato suggested that the Pazzi bank should advance him all the money he needed at a high rate of interest, and let his commitments, public and

The *condottiere* Niccolò da Tolentino painted by Andrea Castagno (*c.* 1423–57) in a fresco in Florence's cathedral. War tended to be a choreographic affair at this time since the *condottieri*, on hire to the state that offered the best terms, avoided quick victories and disliked hurting other *condottieri* to whom they were often related.

private, do the rest. Francesco laughed at him, and Renato thought it wise, seeing that the plot was to go ahead, to retire to the country – not that this saved him later.

The head of the Pazzi family was Jacopo, Francesco's uncle and, according to Luigi Guicciardini, a perfect gentleman, except that he gambled and swore cruelly. According to Lorenzo's Platonist, Agnolo Poliziano, Jacopo played cards night and day, and would 'curse gods and men if he lost, and dash the dice board into the head of the first person who came near him'. He was clearly a good man for a hopeless plot. He had a pale face lined with a strange anxiety, and like his nephew Francesco he was never quiet. He twitched his head constantly and moved his legs about when sitting. Unlike his nephew, he was married, though like him he had no legitimate children. The word *pazzo* in Italian means mad, and historians could be forgiven for thinking that the word derived from the family.

At first, Jacopo scorned the plot, as he tended to scorn most things. Then it worked its subtle enticements on his mind. He announced that he did not like to risk all his wealth on the chance of an assassin's knife, but the Pope's support, and tacit support from King Ferrante in Naples,

the Count of Urbino, Ferrara and Siena made the risk seem worthwhile. And how easy it had been to kill the Duke of Milan! He said he would join the plot on one condition, that no blood was shed. But he would lead the revolution on another condition, that someone else shed the blood. That was the kind of logic he was known for.

In other words the original assassination plot, in all its crudeness, was on. On the face of it, nothing was easier than killing Lorenzo. Unlike the Duke of Milan, he walked about unarmed and unattended. But it was not enough to kill him alone. Giuliano, if anything more popular than he, would simply take the saddle and ride through the city even more successfully as a hero. The two brothers must fall together. Of course, it was not so easy killing two people as killing one, but by dint of planning two simultaneous assassination plots, the difficulties could be overcome. And this was done. Only one of the two succeeded, so that the rest of the plan failed. Then, unlike the murderers of Milan, these plotters did not spend hours rehearsing the scene, for the simple reason that they did not know until the last moment where it was going to take place. As chance would have it, Lorenzo and Giuliano were now always apart, whereas hitherto they had always been together.

The mercenary Montesecco went to Cafaggiolo, one of the Medici seats in the Appenines, to meet Lorenzo, so that he would know his man on the day. Lorenzo received him with that overwhelming sympathy and charm which moved his friends and rankled with his enemies, so much so that the mercenary, who had not even a soldier's grudge against him, began to think twice about his mission. Meanwhile, Francesco de' Pazzi returned to Florence, and Salviati the Archbishop went to Pisa. The plotters decided to use Rafaello Sansoni, a boy-cardinal and nephew of Girolamo, as a decoy. The child happened to be studying at Pisa University and was made to leave the city on the pretext of going to Perugia, of which he had been made governor. He was to stay with Jacopo de' Pazzi in Florence, and, naturally enough, Lorenzo would invite him to dinner. The plotters would come to dinner, for they were sure to be invited too. When he heard of the boy's arrival in Florence, Lorenzo sent a message to the Pazzi house inviting him to dinner at Fiesole, together with other members of his family. The dinner took place but Giuliano de' Medici did not come. He was feeling unwell. The plot was abandoned for that night.

Lorenzo was then told that Rafaello would like to see his collection at the house in Via Larga, and the same guests were promptly invited to that house for the Sunday before Ascension (26 April 1478). They would all attend Mass at the Cathedral, then walk to the house a few hundred yards away. It was decided to kill the brothers as they rose from dinner. The Via Larga house was a convenient place because the plotters could then seize it as a kind of second seat of government. The people of Florence would be called on to join the revolution.

OPPOSITE A portrait of Pierantonio Baroncelli by a fifteenth-century painter of the Flemish school. The Baroncelli were a prominent banking family in Florence, like the Bardi, Peruzzi, Cerchi, Alberi and Medici. All of them combined usury with patronage and charitable works, and Renaissance Florence owes its existence to them.

By this time, the number of plotters involved was enormous, always a drawback. Montesecco brought a troop of twenty Perugian exiles into the city, while the Archbishop of Pisa brought his retinue of Spanish servants. Other discontented people were invited to lend a hand. Bernardo Baroncelli, who had squandered his life away, thought such a plot could only bring him good, since it could not bring him worse than what he had already. Jacopo Bracciolini was the son of a scholar much devoted to the Medici family for having lavished patronage on him. He lacked his father's gifts, while living off them. He had run through his inheritance and, like Baroncelli, was too deeply in debt to care much what happened to him. Napoleone Franzesi of San Gimignano, a supporter of the Pazzi House, joined in. There were also Antonio Maffei of Volterra, who wished to avenge the sack of his city, and Jacopo de' Pazzi's private secretary, a parish priest called Stefano da Bagnone, whose reputation stood even lower than his master's. It was a crew better fitted for fumbling a plot than for running a government.

Everything was set for the Mass and the dinner. Plotters, army and personal bravos were at the ready. The morning came up sunny and tranquil like any other. Then the word went round that Giuliano would not be fulfilling this engagement either. He was now sick in bed. But the two armies were due to arrive at different gates of the city that evening. The plotters saw no way out of their plan. If the two armies retraced their steps, Florence would know all about the plot by dawn next day anyway. The brothers had to be killed. There was a meeting of the chief plotters at the Pazzi house. The deed must be done at Mass, as Giuliano was less likely to yield to persuasions to come to dinner than to Mass. He *must* be got to Mass. Here Montesecco the mercenary looked astonished. At Mass? How could a man be killed at Mass? It appeared that he had a conscience, even a religion! And with an archbishop there to tell him that it was all right, too! He had to be counted out, since he refused to murder in church. It was quickly arranged that the two priests, Antonio Maffei and Stefano da Bagnone, would kill Lorenzo: such a murder could hardly be a sin, being, so to speak, on their own premises.

Francesco de' Pazzi and Bernardo Baroncelli would kill Giuliano. The Archbishop, it was arranged, would leave the cathedral just before the Consecration of the Host, which was to be the signal for the knives to fall. Some witnesses claimed that it happened at another part of the liturgy, at the *Agnus Dei* or the *Ita Missa Est*, but it seems more likely that the Mass bell was the signal, especially as at that moment most people in the church would be stationary in order to make the sign of the cross (it was customary to walk round the church during Mass). The boy Rafaello knew nothing about the plot. Being of tender years and a cardinal, he might have been appalled at a double murder in that place, at that most holy of all moments in the liturgy, and he might have been shocked at the Vicar of Christ being a party to such premeditated blasphemy.

OPPOSITE A portrait of Pierantonio Baroncelli's wife by the same artist.

Rafaello rode to Via Larga, unsuspecting, and changed from his riding clothes in one of the Medici rooms. Lorenzo had already been to church once, and returned to find the boy coming downstairs in his vestments. He accompanied him back to the cathedral. A group of plotters then rode up to the house and asked at the door where Lorenzo and Giuliano were, and were told that they had already gone to church. They rode back to the cathedral, and saw that only Lorenzo had come. Francesco de' Pazzi and Bernardo Baroncelli decided to return to the Via Larga house and persuade Giuliano to come by hook or by crook. He was in bed, but the persuasion worked. His weakness might easily account for the ease with which the two did away with him later. The three then went to the cathedral and walked up the nave together. Francesco was seen to pass his arm round Giuliano's body in a playful way, to find out if he was armed. As it happened, Giuliano had a sore on his leg and had left his dagger behind because it rubbed against it. When everyone was in church, strolling about affably, Archbishop Salviati excused himself and left.

Giuliano and Lorenzo were separate from each other, walking round the high altar with their friends in a clockwise direction. When the moment for the murder came, Giuliano was on the north side of the high altar, that is on its left when seen from the body of the church, while Lorenzo was on the opposite, southern side. Suddenly Baroncelli shouted *'There! Traitor!'* and plunged his dagger into Giuliano's side. Giuliano fell sideways towards Francesco de' Pazzi, who drove a knife deep into his chest. Others of the Pazzi family and their entourage of servants dashed forward and knifed him again and again. He had nineteen wounds on his body. On the other side of the altar, there was confusion. The priest Maffei had put his hand on Lorenzo's shoulder from behind in order to steady himself to deliver a deep wound in his back. Lorenzo had turned at once, and his sword was drawn before the other man could take breath. He also wrapped his cloak round his shoulder to protect himself. Maffei's second effort grazed his neck lightly. Having killed Giuliano, Francesco de' Pazzi and Baroncelli now rushed round the altar to help kill Lorenzo, but by this time two of the Cavalcanti family and some other youths of the Medici party had completely surrounded Lorenzo. Agnolo Poliziano was present too and protected Lorenzo with his body. Another of the Medici men, Francesco Nori, a bank manager whom Lorenzo had often used on diplomatic missions, was stabbed to death by the vicious Baroncelli. Francesco de' Pazzi was wounded in the leg. Lorenzo managed to jump the low rail round the choir, which at that time was made of wood. He ran in front of the high altar, pushed through the wicket of the choir and ran towards the northern sacristy (called the 'new' sacristy or the 'sacristy of the Mass'). He must have run past Giuliano's body without noticing it. He and his followers managed to get inside the sacristy and slam the heavy doors closed. Luca della

Robbia's bronze reliefs on the door (figuring, among other subjects, the Madonna and Child, and Doctors of the Church) saved their lives. They had been completed but ten years before. The Pazzi crowd failed to push them down. The wooden door of the other sacristy would have been down in a moment.

It was all over in a few seconds. Indeed, most of the congregation had no idea what had happened. The terrified Rafaello was cowering in his vestments by the altar. Later, when knives were no longer in evidence, he was led into the other sacristy. Lorenzo's brother-in-law, Guglielmo de' Pazzi, could be heard above the din shouting that he was innocent of any part in the conspiracy. Choristers were running here, there and everywhere. Most of the congregation thought that the roof had fallen in over the altar, as there had recently been much speculation about the safety of the cupola, which Brunelleschi had built according to a new system without supporting arms, as a double vault.

Lorenzo and his followers inside the sacristy were debating what to do. One of the youths, Antonio Ridolfi, sucked the wound in Lorenzo's neck in case the dagger had been poisoned. Meanwhile, there were

Florence's cathedral was begun at the end of the thirteenth century on a design by Arnolfo di Cambio (1240–c. 1302) to replace the old cathedral of S. Reparata, as part of a plan to embellish the increasingly prosperous city. It was completed by Filippo Brunelleschi, who engineered the dome, and Michelozzo (1396–1472), both of them favoured Medici architects.

The interior of the Florentine cathedral.

people outside the sacristy door shouting to be let in and saying they were friends. Another youth, Sigismundi della Stufa, climbed up into the organ gallery above the sacristy door (it is still there) to have a look at them, and saw Giuliano below, lying dead. He confirmed that there were friends outside but said nothing to Lorenzo about his brother. The door was opened and Lorenzo was escorted home under heavy guard, everyone making sure that he did not see Giuliano's corpse.

While this was going on, the Archbishop, Salviati, as always master of the crass move, had got inside the courtyard of the Signoria with thirty of his followers and had asked to speak to the chief justice privately. He walked up the stairs with some of his men while the others secured the door below (little realising that they would not be able to get out again). The priors were at dinner, but the chief justice, Cesare Petrucci, left the dining hall and received Salviati in an anteroom. As luck would have it, Petrucci had lately been involved in the Prato riot, and had learned to be suspicious of sudden callers like the Archbishop. The vestments did not fool him. Salviati did his best to look suspicious anyway. He stuttered, cleared his throat several times and looked anxiously behind him at the door as if he needed the support of his retinue. But his bravos were on the other side of the door below (Petrucci had cleverly fitted it with a spring lock not many days before), and Salviati must have realised that he was without support. The idea was, no doubt, to rush the priors while they were at dinner and massacre the lot. Petrucci suddenly called for the guard. Salviati turned and ran away. Petrucci ran after him and bumped into one of the plotters, called Bracciolini, who seemed to want to fight. Petrucci twisted his hair and then threw him to the ground. The priors and a few attendants came running out at this point. Petrucci ran to the kitchen and seized hold of a great spit while the others pulled the chain across the top of the stairway. A few Perugian soldiers came up but could not get beyond the chain. The Signoria bell began ringing madly, and people started pouring into the square outside. They found the gate locked.

Then the head of the 'revolution' appeared on horseback riding through the crowd, Jacopo de' Pazzi himself, shouting *People and liberty!* at the top of his voice. The priors and their attendants threw stones at him from the windows of the palace, while the people in the square gave him the only suitable answer, *'Balls!'*, meaning the balls of the Medici arms.

Jacopo de' Pazzi, with as many of his retainers as he could find, rode full gallop out of the square towards the Porta Santa Croce and his country seat a mile from the city. The palace gate was forced open by the crowd. The 'strangers' inside were cut down at once, Perugians and Spaniards. Those upstairs were thrown out of the windows. News reached the palace of Giuliano's murder. Francesco de' Pazzi was dragged from his bed, where he was nursing the wound in his leg, and escorted to the palace. Petrucci had a rope tied round his neck, then flung him from a window. Salviati too was seized, roped and thrown out in full vestments to hang at Pazzi's side. The crowd below saw the Archbishop twist himself grotesquely towards Francesco de' Pazzi as he fell, and bite him in the breast, then grip the rope round his neck with his teeth. Two of his men followed him. The people below were screaming

This Pazzi conspiracy medal, struck in 1478, shows (above) a bust of Lorenzo placed above the octagonal choir of Florence's cathedral, inside which Mass is being celebrated, while below, conspirators are attempting to kill him; (below) a bust of Lorenzo's brother Giuliano also above the cathedral choir, while conspirators rain dagger blows on his body below.

'*Balls! Balls!*'. One of them was waving a spit from the palace with a head and genitalia impaled on it. Not one man had cried '*Marzocco!*', meaning the lion of the Florentine arms and support for the Pazzi. Within an hour of the assassination attempt, it was clear that Medici rule was confirmed and guaranteed.

Lorenzo was escorted to the Signoria with a bandage round his neck. He appeared at one of the windows and the crowd roared its approval. He was perhaps not quite happy at the sight of an archbishop dangling below in full vestments, dead now, knowing that he would have to pay dearly for Petrucci's decision, even with his own life. He asked the people below to go home quietly. The young Cardinal, Rafaello, was also escorted through the crowd – who tried to lynch him. Florentines were fond of telling each other in later years how Raffaello never got the colour back into his cheeks after that, and was for ever putting his hand to his neck as if he felt a rope there. Apparently, it did not stop him being one of the hardest gamblers in the Italian peninsula.

Jacopo de' Pazzi was caught two days later. He had ridden on to the Tuscan border, where a peasant recognised him. Jacopo offered the man seven gold crowns if he would kill him there and then, but the peasant simply hit him. He was brought back to Florence, where torture, followed by hanging, awaited him. He told his torturers that Lorenzo's new inheritance law had turned him into a rebel. Poliziano said that before he was executed, Jacopo de' Pazzi screamed out that he offered his soul to the devil. The innocent Renato de' Pazzi was dragged from his country villa and hanged with him. He had disguised himself as a peasant. His brother was hanged naked, he in his disguise.

The crowd pitied Renato, but Lorenzo was implacable. There was a touch of hardness in him, the effect of having power in youth. It had shown itself in his reaction to the Volterra rising, and in his vengeful inheritance law, for which Giuliano, who had protested against it, had now paid with his life. We hear nothing from chroniclers of the time about the effect on Lorenzo of his brother's death, except that he was heart-broken. Most probably it was the reason why he hunted the conspirators to the last man. He had grown up with Giuliano at his side, he had shared problems of government with him, and the murder changed his life. He was never quite the same Lorenzo again. He calculated more than before. In hanging Renato, he was calculating, as were his party chiefs, that such a man, if left alive, might become a serious political rival, being the only popular member of his family. It was a foolish calculation. Renato had been loyal to the Medici interest, and would almost certainly have been more so had he been spared. There is a letter which has survived, from Jacopo de' Pazzi to Lorenzo, testifying to the friendship between the two families, dated only four years before the plot: 'Magnificent Lorenzo, I recommend myself to your good grace. I have been informed of the new budget, and the elections, which

I praise and commend. . . . I have also been told that my own case has been put to you, and that your reply was as gracious and benign as could be.' He went on to talk of Lorenzo's 'supreme integrity and goodness', and thanked God for his safety.

On the other hand, Renato's advice to his brother and uncle to lend Lorenzo large sums of money in order to ruin him had probably come to Lorenzo's ears. We do not know the aftermath of Jacopo de' Pazzi's letter of four years before: it is possible that Lorenzo did not give Jacopo all he wanted, and that resentment began to rankle long before the Pope tried to buy Imola. The Pazzi were, after all, nearer to the Medici in power than any other family. It was a naked struggle for power. Lorenzo must have known that he was provoking open war when he put through his new inheritance law, just as Francesco de' Pazzi must have known that his betrayal of Lorenzo's instructions to the Pope would not go unavenged. The only extraordinary thing is that the Medici did not expect a conspiracy and get wind of it, since Lorenzo had virtually made an open confrontation between the two power-blocs inevitable. Rome and Naples saw him not as the innocent victim of an unprovoked attack but as a wily politician who had started and then won a war for total power.

Lorenzo went out of his way to be kind to the relatives of those who had been put to death. He heard that one Averardo Salviati, brother of the late Archbishop of Pisa, lived in Florence and had hidden himself in his house. He summoned the man to Via Larga and received him with such kindness that Salviati burst into tears. They later became close friends. He also wrote a kindly letter in Latin to Rafaello Mattei, brother of one of the priests who had tried to murder him, in case he too should feel hunted. In due time he released the boy-cardinal.

Naturally, this was the kindness of a man who had triumphed – and who feared papal reprisals. The Pazzi family had hitherto been his most powerful rival. Now it had been wiped off the slate. This meant, from the Pope's point of view, that there was no one to challenge Medici policy, which could be expected to go on coveting papal possessions in the Romagna, and fighting the Curia for possessions like Imola. This is why it seemed to the Pope doubly necessary to get rid of Lorenzo – because there was now no effective opposition to him inside Florence. A few months before, his murder had seemed desirable. Now it was an urgent necessity. And, personally speaking, Sixtus would never forgive him for having exposed his own complicity. It was as bad as facing a General Council of the Church.

On the third day of May, the two priests whose job it had been to kill Lorenzo were found cowering in the Badia. The people wanted to burn the place down right away for sheltering them. Lorenzo never gave it a nice new neo-classical front as he was often asked to. The priests had their ears and noses sliced off and were then handed over for hanging. Montesecco, the mercenary captain, was also caught and tortured. He dictated a full confession to Florence's chancellor, Bartolomeo della Scala. He described how he met Francesco de' Pazzi and Archbishop Salviati in the latter's quarters in Rome: 'The archbishop began speaking about their plan to overturn the state of Florence, and how determined they were to carry it out, and that they wanted my help. I replied that I would do anything for them, but being a soldier in the service of the pope and the Curia, I could not take part. They replied, do you think we would do this without the consent of the Curia?'

The confession saved him from death by hanging. He was given a soldier's death by the sword. In all, between seventy and one hundred people were killed, some of them innocent, most of them not. The walls of the *Podestà* and the Signoria were lined with hanging corpses. Giro- lamo Riario's cross-bowmen were all strung up. Prisoners continued to be thrown from the windows. The crowd below always rushed towards the falling corpse, and soldiers who had been brought in from the hills for the city's defence fought each other to get the dead man's jerkin and stockings. One servant of the Pazzi family was found trembling under a stack of wood in the Signoria itself. He was sent home. Only three men known to be involved in the plot escaped. Napoleone Franzesi of San Gimignano got away with the help of his friend Piero Vespucci, who paid for this with two years in gaol. He was lucky to get off so lightly, since he had shouted 'Up with the Pazzi!' when he saw Giuliano dead, and an hour later was leading a mob to burn down the Pazzi houses.

The whole Pazzi family was disqualified from office for all time. Some of them, who had almost certainly not known about the conspiracy, were sent to the dungeons of the castle in Volterra. The Signoria also gave the order that the survivors of the Pazzi family must change their name. Citizens were forbidden to marry the daughters or sisters of any Pazzi condemned to prison. The Pazzi coat-of-arms was smashed wherever it was found. The tiny *piazza dei Pazzi* had its name changed.

As for Guglielmo, Lorenzo's brother-in-law, known to be innocent but naturally under vague suspicion, he was forbidden to go more than twenty miles outside Florence. This ban was soon lifted. It took a long time for the excitement to die down. The soldiers who had been brought into town roamed around for days more, under the command of the *bargello*. A citizen guard was mounted each night. An invasion was expected, since everyone knew by now that the plot had been hatched in a foreign state and approved by others. As always at such times, super- stition mounted. There was incessant rain and the peasants took it into their heads that this was because Jacopo de' Pazzi had been buried, after his hanging, in the chapel of the Pazzi house in Piazza Santa Croce. They broke down the chapel doors, took the corpse and buried it in the garden. There street urchins dug it up again and dragged it round the streets of Florence for at least a fortnight more. A cord was tied to its neck and they cried, 'Room for the great knight!' They tied the cord to the knocker of

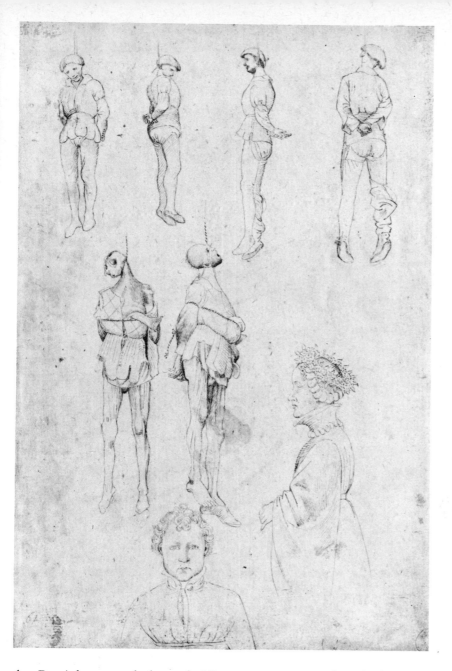

Studies of men hanging by
Antonio Pisanello (1395–1455),
pen and ink over black chalk.
In the Pazzi murder plot
against the Medici in 1478
many of the conspirators were
hanged from the windows of the
Signoria or flung down to the
pavement where their jerkins
and valuables were seized by
peasants and soldiers loyal to
the Medici.

the Pazzi house and shouted, 'Open, your master knocks!' When
Florence was tired of this and the stench became unbearable, it was
thrown into the Arno. Crowds of sightseers on the bridges saw it floating
down the river, its face upwards. At Brozzi, now the western outskirts
of the city, other urchins pulled it ashore, hung it from a willow tree and
flogged it. They then threw it into the water again, and it was later seen
floating through Pisa and out to sea. That was the last of the Pazzi
family. Its possessions, including its stud for thoroughbreds, were con-
fiscated by the state.

The Aftermath

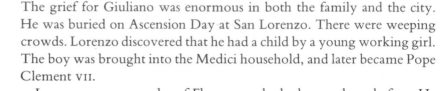

The grief for Giuliano was enormous in both the family and the city. He was buried on Ascension Day at San Lorenzo. There were weeping crowds. Lorenzo discovered that he had a child by a young working girl. The boy was brought into the Medici household, and later became Pope Clement VII.

Lorenzo was now ruler of Florence as he had never been before. He was richer by Giuliano's property. It was clear that neither the people nor his party would refuse him anything. He had the chance of becoming a tyrant. He did not take it. But he did tighten his régime in such a way that the Medici looked like staying for good. The 1478 conspiracy made Grand Dukes out of the Medici in the following century. Everywhere, even in his household, Lorenzo was treated rather like a prince now, since the assassination attempt had been on a princely scale. He no longer walked about the streets unarmed but with a bodyguard of several men, one of whom, walking before him, had his sword drawn.

The affair caused a great stir everywhere in Italy, but especially at the Vatican. In his heart of hearts, Sixtus IV regretted the whole thing, but now that he had a pretext for being angry with Lorenzo (the hanging of an archbishop), he was almost obliged politically to use it for his own ends. Both Girolamo Riario and the King of Naples argued that priests should not be killed even in self defence. Also a cardinal, they added, the young Rafaello, was still held in Florence. The Archbishop had even been hanged in his vestments. How could such a violation of the Church go unpunished?

No one, of course, forgot that two priests had tried to murder Lorenzo in church, and that his brother had been murdered at the Consecration of the Host. Girolamo Riario, the cause of all the trouble, decided to take matters into his own hands, and with three hundred men, arrested the Florentine ambassador in Rome, Donato Acciaiuoli. He was brought before the Pope, but spoke his mind so forcefully that Sixtus became rather embarrassed and rebuked Girolamo for interfering. Meanwhile, the Venetian and Milanese ambassadors swore that if Acciaiuoli went to prison they would follow him. So Sixtus let him go. But Florentine merchants were arrested in both Rome and Naples. Again, those taken in Rome were released, in case the young Cardinal Riario should be used as a hostage for them. Besides, too much money came from Florence, or might be needed, for a quarrel with her merchants to be convenient. Sixtus tried a more subtle line. He announced that he had no quarrel with Florence or her people, only with Lorenzo. He ex-

A medallion showing Lorenzo de' Medici by Niccolò Fiorentino.

communicated him, together with his staunchest supporters. Florence must surrender Lorenzo and these men to the Vatican, on pain of being excommunicated too, together with Pisa and Pistoia. He hoped in this way to divide the people from the Medici, and the subject-towns from Florence. It did not work.

A warm letter, dated 12 May 1478, came from Louis XI to the Via Larga house as if it were the seat of government:

Louis by the grace of God King of France: Dearest friends, we have just heard of the great inhuman outrage, shame and injury which has recently befallen Your Lords, as to the persons of our dear and loved cousins Lorenzo and Giuliano de' Medici, and their friends and relatives, servants and colleagues by the Pazzi; and also the death of our said cousin Giuliano de' Medici, about which we were and are sadder than can be imagined; and because your honour and ours have been so greatly offended; and because the Medici are our relatives, friends and colleagues, and because we look on the said outrage and the death of our said cousin Giuliano the same as if it were done and committed on our own person, and for this reason all the said Pazzi are guilty of treason; we, far from wanting to see the matter go unpunished, feel with all our heart that it must be punished and corrected as an example to all others. And we thought of sending to Your Lords our beloved and faithful Counsellor and Lord in Waiting Signor d'Argentona, steward of our province of Poitou, one of our men in whom we have the greatest confidence, in order to make our intentions known to you at length, and to explain further matters touching on this one. We pray you to believe everything he tells you on our behalf as if it came from our person, because we are sending him to you with precisely this in mind. Praying God, dearest friends, to keep watch over you. Louis.

Meanwhile, Lorenzo was preparing for the war which Louis had in mind. Montesecco's confession had already made it clear that the Pope was out for his blood, by conspiracy or war. The two armies which were to have occupied the city for the Pazzi had turned back and reached the Tuscan frontier, though with some difficulty. But they would soon be used again. Lorenzo knew too that the King of Naples and his son the Duke of Calabria, despite their former love for him and his own close friendship with Federigo and the Duchess, were on the Pope's side. He wrote to every Court in Italy to put his point of view, adding that nothing could be worse for the other Italian states than a revolution in Florence. He wrote Louis XI a long letter of reply in Latin, and also one to the King of Spain.

Simultaneously, he had the word spread through every street in the city that an invasion was imminent. Citizens must prepare to fight. He gathered as much food in the warehouses as they could hold. He worked night and day, and his example was like a stimulant for those round him.

Giovanni Bentivoglio of Bologna was already in the Mugello, north of Florence, with his army, ready to protect the Medici. Ercole d'Este, the Duke of Ferrara, also brought down a formidable army. Venice

A detail from a fresco by Melozzo da Forlì showing Pope Sixtus IV, a Franciscan of humble Genoese origin who worked hard to hoist his family into the aristocracy. He regarded Lorenzo as his principal Italian enemy and was deeply involved in the Pazzi conspiracy.

OPPOSITE A portrait of Giuliano de' Medici, victim of the Pazzi conspiracy, by Sandro Botticelli (1445–1510).

OVERLEAF Botticelli's *Primavera* or *Spring* was commissioned by Lorenzo di Pierfrancesco de' Medici, Lorenzo's second-cousin. Botticelli's paintings were often allegorical, and the meaning of this one is still a matter of dispute.

nodded encouragement, not wanting to get embroiled with Naples or the Pope at this moment. The King of Spain, Ferdinand, returned a warm reply. Louis XI sent Philippe de Commines to Florence and then to Milan, where he persuaded the young Duke on Louis's behalf to send a small army down to Florence. Neither his presence (since he had only his retinue and no money with him) nor the Milanese army made much of an impression on the Florentines, but even honeyed words were useful for morale. Lorenzo began to look strong again even to those in his party who were beginning to think that the Medici sun might be setting.

Sixtus put his anger on record in a ten-page diatribe '*ad futuram rei memoriam*'. It began with the words '*Iniquitatis filius & perditionis alumnus Laurentius de Medicis, & nonnulli alii cives Florentini, ejus in hac parte complices & fautores . . .*': Lorenzo was the 'child of iniquity and the nursling of perdition', together with the citizens of Florence who had helped him. Sixtus compared his own pontifical character, which was gentle and mild, with that of the Florentine fiend, and declared that he would have gone on suffering the insults of his enemies with his usual forbearance had not this Medici abandoned his fear of God and given way to the devil by laying violent hands on the clergy, hanging an archbishop and imprisoning a cardinal.

Lorenzo wrote to the King of France that the thing he seemed to have done wrong in the Pope's eyes was not to be murdered! To most of the Italian and European Courts, he sent a copy of Montesecco's confession, which did nothing to soothe Sixtus's nights.

While excommunicating Lorenzo, the chief justice and other of the city magistrates, the Pope also suspended the clergy inside Florentine territory from the exercise of their spiritual functions. They were indignant, and got together under the Bishop of Arezzo, Gentile Becchi, Lorenzo's old teacher, to prepare a much longer and equally angry indictment of the Pope in eleven closely-argued parts. It condemned Sixtus as the chief instigator of the conspiracy, and absolved Lorenzo and the citizens of Florence from all blame. The papal interdict was declared to be null and void, and the clergy of Florence were directed to administer the sacraments as usual. Louis XI too threatened the Pope – with a General Council of the Church (every pope's nightmare). The King also summoned a synod of the French clergy which froze revenues to Rome. In fact, as Lorenzo was the first to realise, Louis was playing a double game, and found the dismemberment of Florence no less attractive than did most other princes.

Alfonso, Duke of Calabria, sent Florence an ultimatum: if the city yielded Lorenzo to the Pope, she would be received back into the Church, otherwise it was war. Knowing the power of an Interdict on the popular imagination, Lorenzo decided to call the city's most important citizens to the Signoria and put the matter to them. His speech made him more popular than ever, and showed that it was impossible to divide

LAVRENTIVS MEDICES PETRI FILIVS.

Medici interests from the city's. He opened by saying that he had no wish to call up cruel memories of the recent past. He wanted them to be forgotten. But it grieved him that the Pope should descend to persecuting a single individual when Christianity had so much else to think about (he meant the Turks), and to wage war on a state that had done so much for him. Within himself, he added, two feelings were struggling – gratitude for the protection his city had given him, and sorrow that by another's guilt he was the cause of the city's present troubles, for he loved Florence more than his own life. If the city thought that his death or exile would serve the public safety, he was only too happy to offer himself, his property, even the blood of his children freely and frankly to the country. The answer was unanimous. Lorenzo the Magnificent must live and die with the Republic. A guard of twelve outriders was then appointed to guard his person.

And then the war was forgotten. The annual feast of San Giovanni had been postponed to 5 July, but it was then celebrated with a vengeance. There were men dressed as giants and demons and women. Horses raced down the streets in the city's *palio*. The entire city danced and sang. It was clearly to celebrate the state's survival. But, underneath, everyone was anxious. Lorenzo smiled but he had not long since lost his brother. And the war would come. Florence was not prepared, despite adequate food supplies. She had no army.

The first raids by the Sienese (always ready to twist the Florentine tail) caused fantastic panic. Peasants rushed to get within the city walls. There were a few Milanese soldiers about but no allied army. Yet the Neapolitan and papal armies were already in force on the frontier. The attack would come either from Chiusi along the Chiana valley or in a straight line from Siena to Florence through Poggibonsi. In the first case, the enemy would keep to the easily-defended towns of Montepulciano, Sinalunga and Monte San Savino, but the disadvantages were that Arezzo, too big to capture, would lie in the rear of the advance and that the valley was malarial. The second line of advance looked like the

OPPOSITE A retrospective portrait of Lorenzo de' Medici, by Bronzino, one of the Florentine artists patronised by the later Medici dukes.

BELOW The annual feast of San Giovanni, a panel from a fifteenth-century marriage chest. The baptistry of Florence cathedral appears on the left.

obvious one, since Empoli, in the plain north of Poggibonsi, was Florence's granary and not difficult to capture. The advance would also be through Sienese territory, reckoned to be friendly. A revolt could be stirred up in Volterra. Pisa and Livorno would be taken, and Florence cut off from the sea. The Neapolitan fleet would be waiting at anchor to contact an army raised by Ludovico Sforza (one of the brothers exiled from Milan and now a dangerously active enemy of Florence) and his friends in Genoa, the Fregosi family, assembling at this moment in the Lunigiana country north of Pisa. But there were disadvantages here too – that some of the Sienese towns, like Castellina and Colle val d'Elsa and San Gimignano, might not prove friendly towards papal or Neapolitan troops.

At first, the Duke of Calabria and the newly-created Duke of Urbino (now fighting on his side) chose the former route. On 11 July they crossed the Florentine border just below Montepulciano. The meagre Florentine forces retreated on Arezzo, unable to face an army three times as powerful. But then the route was abandoned. To everyone's surprise, the Neapolitans turned a flank westwards which began advancing across the hills towards the Elsa valley, taking Castellina and Rada. Jacopo and Luigi Guicciardini, in charge of Florentine operations, checked this by concentrating a force at Poggio Imperiale, a fortress high above Poggibonsi which commanded the valley north to Florence. Milanese troops had now been joined by Venetians, for Lorenzo. The Marquis of Saluzzo brought up his Alpine infantry which had landed at Pisa, while Ercole d'Este, the Duke of Ferrara, became commander-in-chief of the operation. Movements were slow, due to the summer heat. The Ten of War decided that 27 September was astrologically the best day for Lorenzo to hand over the baton of command to Ercole, and 10.30 in the morning the best hour.

The right flank of the Neapolitan army was meanwhile laying siege to Monte San Savino, below Arezzo. Ercole was ordered to relieve it but he was a leisurely man and started to move only when it was capitulating.

Things were definitely not going well for Florence. And the danger for Lorenzo was that the Florentines, as ungrateful a lot as in Dante's time, would begin to identify their misfortunes with his name, particularly as they had an Interdict hanging over them. Worse news arrived. King Ferrante helped the exiled Doge of Genoa, Ludovico Fregoso, to reinstate himself: he did this by reconciling the Adorni and Fregosi families which had been at each other's necks for generations. It meant that the Milanese army could now be attacked in force, and this was done by the exiled Sforza brothers and their cousin Ruberto San Severino. Naturally, most of the Milanese pulled out of the Florentine front. It was far worse than losing a few towns in Sienese territory. The Duchess of Milan surrendered the fortress of Castelletto, which the Milanese had taken from Genoa, to one of the Fregosi brothers, Battista, who had decided that the recent settlement engineered by Ferrante was not to his liking. Having got the fortress, he pressed on into Genoa and expelled both Prospero Adorno and the Doge Ludovico Fregoso. At this rate, the Duchess of Milan, advised by Cecco Simonetta, would not be on her throne for much longer.

Naples now commanded the Mediterranean coast, as far as Florence's outlets were concerned. There was a popular riot against Florence at Lucca, and Piero Capponi, the *Podestà*, was almost killed. Only the intervention of the French ambassador stopped Lucca from declaring war on Florence: he threatened to freeze Lucchese merchandise in France. At Pistoia, on Florence's doorstep, a plot engineered by Alfonso, Duke of Calabria, was uncovered only just in time.

The plague suddenly hit Florence. Seven or eight people were dying every day. Trade had slumped, and without that the Florentine was listless and pessimistic. A number of men were hanged for plundering near the Porta San Niccolò, masquerading as a Neapolitan raiding party. Factory-owners were locking out their workers, particularly in the silk and wool industries. As always at such times, people were impressionable. They were much taken by a man who wandered into the city from Volterrano, young and spare, with only a bag on his back, prophesying disaster from the steps of the Signoria, before the Eight of Watch and Ward sent him away.

It looked as if Lorenzo would have to sue for peace. One of the prizes asked would certainly be his own person. As always, Florentine diplomacy did what the armies could not do. Lorenzo sent Tommaso Soderini to Venice and Girolamo Morelli to Milan to plead for more support. Soderini asked the Venetians to attack Imola so that the Duke of Urbino would be drawn away from the Chiana valley, that is the approaches to Florence along the Cassian way. Also they should launch a naval attack on the Neapolitan coast. At Milan it was decided that Ridolfo Gonzaga, brother of the Marquis of Mantua, should be sent down to help the Duke of Ferrara hold the Elsa valley.

Venice sent their mercenary captain Ruberto Malatesta to help Carlo Fortebraccio to start trouble in Fortebraccio's home town, Perugia, to divert papal troops, and also act as a rearguard nuisance against the right flank of the Neapolitans. The plan failed because Fortebraccio died. His son took over, however, and with Malatesta he threw a small army against papal troops on the shores of Lake Trasimene and routed them. He then pressed on to Perugia, pillaging every farmhouse on the way. This created a diversion. Neapolitan forces moved away from the Monte San Savino area to deal with Fortebraccio and Malatesta, and this helped the Florentines in their attack on Casole from their Poggio Imperiale above Poggibonsi. But the attacking force, consisting of Mantuan and Ferrarese troops, started quarrelling about booty, and had to be separated by a third contingent.

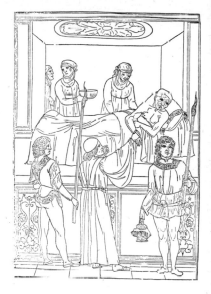

An illustration from 1493, showing a plague doctor smelling an amber apple to avoid infection while treating a stricken patient.

Ridolfo Gonzaga was sent over towards Perugia to reinforce the army under Malatesta, while Costanzo Sforza, lord of Pesaro on the Adriatic coast, helped Sigismondo d'Este to hold the Elsa valley. The positions here were not strong, and the Neapolitans were quick to see it. They called in their dispersed forces in the area and advanced up the Arbia river from Chiusi. One morning, before dawn, they stormed Poggio Imperiale, which was virtually undefended (the Florentines were not expecting an attack). A good number of men were taken prisoner, including some of the mercenary officers. Meanwhile, Costanzo Sforza on the east flank of the Neapolitan forces had Jacopo d'Appiano, lord of Piombino, at his heels, but he suddenly turned round and took him prisoner. This surprise action saved the day. He rallied the broken forces at Casciano, which was enough to plant a strong line of troops across the Elsa valley.

But Florence was open to the enemy. However, the Duke of Calabria chose not to advance up the Cassian way. He sat down in front of Colle val d'Elsa instead, and Florence was inexplicably saved. That little town was put under the command of a Venetian mercenary and withstood attack after attack. Meanwhile, Florentine troops came from San Gimignano to worry the Neapolitan rear. The Duke of Calabria was a rash man. It took him two months to break Colle val d'Elsa and by that time (November 1479) the morale of his troops was as low as his supplies, and he sued for a three-month truce. Perhaps he had calculated that it was too late in the year for a long advance on Florence followed by a major siege. Or perhaps the King of Naples did not seriously want Florence to fall: that way, the Pope might have become too strong.

The fall of Colle created panic in Florence. Also, every village churchbell in the Mugello began ringing after news arrived that Girolamo Riario was leading an army down from Imola across the Apennines towards Florence. Those families which had fled from the plague in the city now began to wish themselves back, plague or no plague. But here again Florence's luck was in. The Duke advanced only twenty or so miles to just within the Tuscan border, and he sat down in Piancaldoli. It really did look as if Naples wanted to frighten, but not ruin, the Medici state.

Not that any Florentine felt safe, particularly when news came that the Pope had persuaded Swiss troops on contract to Milan to disregard their contract and swarm over the St Gothard pass to capture Bellinzona and make ugly faces southwards. Ruberto San Severino and the exiled Sforza brothers had already threatened Pisa at the beginning of the year, and had been stopped only by the timely arrival of the Duke of Ferrara. Then the country round Parma was almost lost to them. Luckily for Milan, the Sforza brothers were afraid of being trapped in the mountains and retreated to the Lunigiana, where one of them died. San Severino and Ludovico Sforza (nicknamed *Il Moro* or 'the Moor') then seized

RIGHT A wooden
Florentine shield from the
middle of the fifteenth century.
Painted with the arms of the
Villanis, an old Florentine
family, it is the kind used in
military parades and pageants
rather than in actual fighting.

BELOW Italian helmets
from the second half of
fifteenth century.

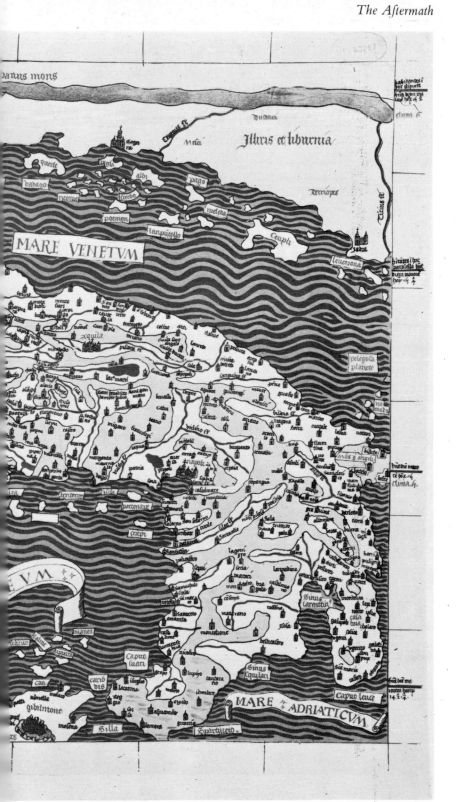

A map of Italy, dated 1480–5,
which was probably executed,
as part of a general map of
Europe, for the Archduke
Maximilian, whose borrowings
from the Medici helped to
wreck the Bruges branch of
the Medici bank.

Tortona in the Po valley, and announced that they wished to conduct a war of liberation on Milan: the young Duke of Milan must be wrested from the clutches of his mother and that hated confidant Cecco Simonetta. The Duchess managed the invasion well by opening the gates to Ludovico and allowing him a triumphal entry. She was removed politely from the government of Milan, and Simonetta, chief advocate of the Florentine alliance, was gaoled at Pavia.

At no time did Lorenzo take a leading part in the campaign, and no one expected him to. He did, however, visit headquarters. Fighting, or seeming to one's employer to fight, was a matter of politics and not heroism. Battles were won with money, dynastic agreement and diplomatic skill. Lorenzo was needed to take charge of those three things in Florence. The basic distress was financial. If trade diminished and threatened Florence's credit-position, there was no further hope for the city: it would be able neither to pay the mercenary captains their bills, nor to convince other Courts that Florence was worth fighting for. The longer the war went on, the worse Florence's position became.

The mercenary captains were only too happy: as usual, they insisted on at least four months in winter quarters. None of them seemed to want to win. Federigo of Urbino clearly wanted to harm his son-in-law, Ruberto Malatesta, on the other side, as little as Alfonso, Duke of Calabria wanted to hurt his brother-in-law Ercole d'Este, or Costanzo Sforza his relative Ludovico. The fighting was at times much stronger inside the camps than in battle. The Mantuans and Ferrarese were always brawling on points of booty, their commanders on points of military doctrine. One thing united both soldiers and commanders, and that was dislike of the so-called commissioners who were in charge of the operations and the money: they were invariably civilians who knew little about war and even less about the subtle points of honour which kept mercenary armies dallying with each other for weeks on end. This is why Florence did far less well than it need have done in the war: the Neapolitans were in the service of their own king and not on mercenary contract; they had no need of commissioners appointed by the home government.

Again, Lorenzo was saved by foreigners. The war was beginning to attract the attention of every Court north of the Alps, understandably since the Turks were advancing through Hungary, and Venice was forced to negotiate a peace with the Sultan. It was clearly no time to have Italy divided. The French had for some time been trying to persuade the Pope to meet his enemy at a conference in Lyons. Sixtus almost told the envoys to their faces that this was impertinence. But he did nominate a committee of cardinals to look into the possibilities of a peaceful settlement. He climbed down over Lorenzo's person, and demanded instead the person of Niccolò Vitelli, who had stirred up so much trouble in Città di Castello under Lorenzo's protection. He also insisted that Lorenzo give up Borgo San Sepulcro, which he had on lease, and the nearby townships. He must also pay an indemnity. They were tough terms, and deliberately so, as he hoped Lorenzo would turn them down. He did. Besides, Sixtus was going through the motions of sueing for peace only to stop Louis XI disturbing his nights with suggestions of a General Council. Finally these suggestions became so hot that he agreed to let France, together with England, arbitrate with Lorenzo on his behalf: and if their efforts failed, the Emperor Frederick III and his son Maximilian were to take over.

It would have helped Lorenzo far more had Louis XI sent him the five hundred lances he had long ago promised him. But Louis needed these to fight the Emperor, in an effort to push France's border with the empire further east. Lorenzo bribed French envoys passing through the city as hard as he could but, as he well knew, it was useless. He and Louis remained good friends, and it was still possible to frighten the Pope with the thought of French intervention. Official good relations with France never waned, and in Louis's last years there was a constant stream of letters from Paris to Florence asking little favours such as 'a big dog to guard my person' or the bones of St Bernard or the ring of St Zenobius or medals struck at Pisa with the image of the Virgin which were said to relieve arthritis or a certain doctor called 'the Turk' who was skilled in purgatives.

Lorenzo had been beaten. The war was ruining his city. Even his prestige was crumbling at the edges. In a short time, Florence would find it commercially more valuable to be without the Medici. Even his trusted allies were negotiating with the enemy. In an effort to persuade the Pope to call the Swiss mercenaries off the borders, the Milanese had started talking to King Ferrante. The Pope was told by everyone round him that Lorenzo would be finished in a matter of weeks. The plague had not abated in Florence. At one moment, there was the glimmer of a hope for Florence that Sixtus would die, as he was desperately sick. But the news from the battle fronts was a blood transfusion for the old pontifical war-horse, and he was soon up again.

The Master-stroke of Lorenzo's Career

Quite unexpectedly, Lorenzo threw himself on the mercy of the King of Naples. He must for long have seen that the weakest point on the enemy side was the alliance between Naples and the Vatican. It may even have seemed to him, or perhaps he got wind of the fact, that Naples wanted to tame but not maim him. By suddenly taking the initiative, he made himself famous everywhere in Europe as the master-mind of contemporary politics.

He never lacked that sense of the dramatic which is so essential in politics. He did not ask anyone's permission to go. He announced his decision to only forty of the city's most prominent citizens whom he called together on 5 December 1479. He told them that he would put to the test the enemy's claim that the war was against him and not Florence by offering himself up to them. Rather wisely, considering that the state was on the edge of bankruptcy, the forty men said nothing against the idea. It was a brave move, not simply because Lorenzo was about to walk into the enemy camp, but because King Ferrante had shown that one might enter his palace with a safe conduct, as poor Piccinino the *condottiere* had done, and come out on a bier.

OPPOSITE Botticelli's *Pallas and the Centaur*, an allegorical painting said to represent Lorenzo's triumph over his enemies after his return from Naples in 1480. Pallas, the goddess of wisdom, has Lorenzo's private crest, three interlaced rings, as the motif on her dress. Pallas Athene was a favourite subject of Lorenzo.

BELOW Another lunette from the Palazzo Vecchio painted by Vasari in the sixteenth century. It shows Lorenzo embracing the King of Naples.

On the other hand, there was nothing rash about what he did. It was the result of careful calculation. He and his state were hopeless at war. In one way, he shone above every other man in the Signoria, including his ablest diplomatists, and that was in the capacity to persuade. He meant to persuade the King of Naples that the papal kiss of friendship was really the kiss of death, and that without the strength of both Florence and Milan in the north there would be nothing to stop the Pope occupying all central Italy and then, perhaps with foreign help, pushing the Aragonese out of their Italian possessions. Lorenzo knew that he had two friends close to the Neapolitan King who would sing for him when his voice got dry – the Duchess of Calabria and the King's son Federigo. He would also have much to say about current Italian politics for the very reason that he knew more about them than anyone else, as his grandfather Cosimo had done. He could point out that no pope was a reliable ally because he changed sides too quickly; in the few years between his election and his death, the pope naturally worked hard for his own family, to secure it future positions of power, precisely as Sixtus was working for his army of nephews, notably Pietro and Girolamo Riario. Lorenzo would also tell him that it was useless forming a new alliance with Milan as Ludovico *il Moro* was an adventurer and not a statesman of the calibre of Filippo Maria Visconti or Francesco Sforza. And then, would Louis XI allow Florence to die? Would he not at the last moment tear himself away from his battles on the Rhine to rescue his best ally in the Italian peninsula? In any case, would Louis leave Florence's destruction unavenged? Would he not take up the old Anjou claim to the throne of Naples? And what about Venice – surely she had made peace with the Turks in order to deal with the Pope? And would not the Serenissima perhaps invite the Turks to sweep down on those Neapolitan ports whose vulnerability so disturbed the King? And he was obliged to point out that his own influence with the Turks was very great (and indeed this one fact may have weighed with Naples more than any other).

A few days before he called the forty citizens to his house, Lorenzo had sent Filippo Strozzi off to Naples as an advance envoy. He already had word from Ferrante himself that a visit from him would be welcome. But Strozzi, when he arrived in Naples, had no idea that Lorenzo himself intended to come. The King told him at his first audience. Lorenzo left Florence in great secrecy the day after his meeting with the forty men, that is on 6 December. Only when he reached Samminiato dei Tedeschi, on his way to the coast, did he send official word back that he was on his way, having calculated that 'it was better for one man to risk his life than the whole state'. By this time, two Neapolitan galleys were waiting for him at anchor outside Vada, between Castiglioncello and Cecina. He set sail on 11 December. It had all been done with remarkable speed. Within a week he was in Naples harbour, with royal ships coming out to meet him, and a party at the quay to embrace him – Don Federigo and the

Duke of Calabria's younger son, Ferrantino. There were sightseers too. It was the arrival of a great prince.

He was soon installed in a palace opposite the King's at Castel Nuovo. It took three months of talking to break Ferrante's papal affiliations down. The King's chief counsellor, Diomede Carafa, Count of Maddaloni, also a friend of Lorenzo's, helped with arguments of his own. The Duchess of Calabria added her persuasions. The King called her Lorenzo's 'ally', smilingly. He listened, temporised, gave no indication of what his final decision would be. It ought to have been a restful period for Lorenzo after the months of anxiety at Florence. But he was in a torture of doubt. He did take long hours off with his friends, and wrote poetry. He strolled with the Duchess in the marvellous gardens that sloped down to the Chiaia. It was spring for Naples and everything was in bud. And at that time Naples was one of the most cultivated cities in Europe, with a life as generous and stimulating as Florence's, without the rather chill commercial accompaniment. And it was full of Tuscans anyway. It had been for generations. Bankers, scholars, painters had emigrated there, drawn by the late King Alfonso's splendidly literate Court. Lorenzo gave sumptuous banquets. He endeared himself to the people usefully by giving dowries to needy girls, and procuring the release of galley slaves. Along the coast there were plenty of amusements: in this respect, life had not changed much since the decline of the Roman empire, when that part of Italy had been famous for its fleshpots.

A view of Naples and her bay, with Vesuvius in the right distance. It was here that Lorenzo the Magnificent landed in 1480 when he made his desperate diplomatic journey to see the King of Naples, Ferrante. He dissuaded the unpredictable Ferrante from backing Sixtus IV in the Pope's war against Florence.

145

Storm in an enclosed bay by Leonardo da Vinci. The castle nestled against the rocks gives a glimpse of the elegance of the Renaissance.

OPPOSITE The fifteenth-century triumphal arch of the warlike Alfonso I of Aragon, who invaded Naples and made himself king, leaving the throne to his bastard son Ferrante at his death.

Lorenzo had plenty to do, working and entertaining and making love, but even so he had many hours alone, feeling rather like a prisoner whose trial had yet to come. He knew that the Duchess's husband was no 'ally' as she was, and that the Pope was busy sending down messages to the King that he must on no account give way to Lorenzo's blandishments. Lorenzo was prepared to go to Rome to 'bend the knee' to Sixtus, but King Ferrante warned him that this was not safe.

There was more distressing news from Florence. Venice pretended to withdraw her mercenaries in annoyance with Lorenzo for having separate talks. His Romangnolo allies, small lords who had everything to gain from a war against the Pope and everything to lose from peace, were distinctly worried. Ten of them got together under Agnolo della

Stufa and wrote to Lorenzo that they depended on his honour. Every day, more people seemed to depend on Lorenzo to get a good deal for them. It was not easy, especially as his own city was now taking the attitude that he must secure a treaty without ceding a metre of Florentine territory. He heard too that the two Fregosi brothers had surprised Sarzana near Pietrasanta, one of his proudest acquisitions. It was now in their hands. The story went round Naples that the Duke of Calabria had tipped them off to do this. In enemy hands, Sargana would stop help reaching Florence from Milan, and if Milan became an enemy too, it would make Florence's collapse doubly certain. He heard that while Florence itself was in quite a hopeful mood, one or two prominent people were saying that from now on, the city should be in the hands of 'more than one man'.

King Ferrante agreed to peace at the end of February. Sixtus was furious, but by this time Lorenzo was at sea. The bells of Florence rang for his arrival, and happy crowds lined the streets. Peace was proclaimed on the Feast of the Annunciation: the Madonna of Imprunetta was carried into the city before a splendid procession. Lorenzo had worked hard to achieve such a diplomatic victory and his reward was the gratitude and admiration of the war-weary people of Florence.

Besides needing an ally against too strong (or too fickle) a pope, King Ferrante probably knew that Lorenzo would be prepared to turn Italian politics upside down to save Florence, and that Venice would be behind him. The Serenissima had already lost her possessions in the Morea to the Turks, and might look for a compensating hold in southern Italy: she was not above using Turkish attacks on southern ports to cover her own designs. A real disruption of Italy seemed feasible, and even the Pope must have seen that the Turks might overrun the peninsula, to face not an allied Italian army but the French. Yet King Ferrante seems to have had regrets within a few hours of his agreement, for he sent a message to Lorenzo, who was already at sea, that he would be grateful if he returned to Naples at once. Lorenzo did not do so. He had an idea that Ferrante had been in touch with the Pope, and had finally been swayed against him.

The peace-conditions were not too bad. Monte San Savino, Colle Val d'Elsa, Poggibonsi, Castellina and various other towns in the Chiana valley were to be ceded to Siena. That was really not tragic, as it would be only a matter of time getting them back. Worse was the fact that Sarzana did not figure in the terms at all. King Ferrante guaranteed the safety of the trembling lordlings of the Romagna against the Pope. He insisted that those members of the Pazzi family still imprisoned at Volterra must be released, and this Lorenzo did at once and most willingly. There was to be no indemnity, but a *condotta* or annual payment of the kind made to mercenary captains was to be granted to the unscrupulous Duke of Calabria.

OPPOSITE Florence's Palazzo Vecchio or Signoria. This was the traditional seat of government during the republic, and is today the town hall.

This view of Volterra, one of Florence's subject towns in the fifteenth century, shows the baptistry and dome of the cathedral, which was built in the tenth century and restored in the thirteenth. When Volterra rebelled from Florentine rule in 1470 over its alum mines, Lorenzo de' Medici subdued the town ruthlessly.

The Pope was obliged to proclaim the peace in Rome because without Ferrante he could not fight. But he refused to lift the Interdict against Lorenzo and his government, despite the ardent persuasions of the Florentine ambassador. He insisted that Lorenzo come to Rome in person. This Lorenzo would probably have done had it not been for a second warning that his life would not be safe, this time from the Duke of Ferrara.

His position in Florence was still not firm, despite his popularity. New taxes had to be imposed. Thousands of florins were required to pay off the armies and then finance the peace. The Venetians now cooled towards both Florence and Milan, and made a separate treaty with the Pope. The Duke of Calabria and his army were still lingering in the Chiana valley on the pretence that the Duke of Lorraine, grandson of King René, was threatening a new invasion of Naples. It soon became clear that the Duke was determined to take a slice of Tuscany for himself. He worked on Sienese hatred for Florence, handing out money to the leading men of that republic. He was soon popular. At the same time he encouraged the old noble families of the city to overthrow the government, which they did. Monte de' Nove, with Neapolitan troops behind him, seized Siena's piazza. It looked as if the Duke had a firm base from which to launch an attack on the rest of Tuscany. Things did not look bright for Lorenzo after the merriment had died down.

The Turks saved him again, whether or not by previous arrangement with him we do not know. Their fleet attacked Otranto on 6 August 1480, and beseiged it. King Ferrante ordered the Duke of Calabria to return at once.

The Turkish attack had nothing hit-and-run about it. Otranto was stormed by seven thousand men. Turkish divisions were also forming up in Albania. There was talk of their trying to march on Rome from the south. The Venetians were suspected of having a finger in all this, largely because the Turkish fleet had passed the Venetian island of Corfu unharmed and unhindered. But those who knew more about Italian politics pointed at Lorenzo. He had mentioned his influence with the Turks to Ferrante. No doubt this was his answer to the Duke of Calabria's takeover of Siena. And it worked.

Even Sixtus was forced to climb down. At the end of 1480, he received a Florentine embassy in place of Lorenzo's person. Lorenzo gave this embassy strict instructions not to offer money to the Pope or to stay in Rome, unless they and Florence were offered absolution. The embassy met Sixtus on the first Sunday of Advent on the steps of St Peter's – and on their knees. Luigi Guicciardini, now an old man, spoke for them. Sixtus gave them a talking-to from the papal throne under the portico, since the party could not enter church before being cleaned of their sins. He did not ask them to bare their backs for symbolic chastisement as he might have done. In his mind he no doubt heard the rumbling of Turkish artillery in the south. Instead of chastising, he touched each envoy on the shoulder with his staff as he came near, and made him repeat after him the words '*Miserere mei Deus*'. Then he gave them his blessing. The bronze gates were flung open and the procession entered, with the Pope going before, held aloft on his chair. There was a great crowd. High Mass was celebrated. It could hardly be heard for the mob outside who were screaming abuse at the Florentine dogs; having no doubt been rehearsed and paid by Girolamo Riario. The absolution was a great load off Lorenzo's shoulders, despite Sixtus's demand that he should fit out fifteen galleys to fight the Turks. He was safe again in his own city.

Part Four

Lorenzo and the Renaissance

Lorenzo had come through, and he had also been broken in as a ruler. He was thirty-two years old. He had been ruthless as well as kind. He had learned that he either fought hard for the Medici interest or lost it. The recent war had taught him that the deepest friendships meant nothing when it came to the clash of interests. Don Federigo had not saved him from Ferrante, nor the Duchess from her own husband. They had served him well in Naples only when Ferrante's interests had veered towards saving Florence rather than dismembering her. Lorenzo had used the Turks as many an adventurer before and after him. It was not an easy life, particularly after a youth spent in the atmosphere of a Platonic 'academy' discussing the future civilisation based on that 'perfect man' of the Jews and that other 'perfect man' of the Greeks. The more the Middle Ages fell behind in the shadows, the more power seemed at variance with perfection. The Turks and money saved Florence, and its thought and art and gaiety of disposition began to seem something not only apart but irrelevant.

But his old life continued, perhaps more ardently for having been threatened. In 1480 he bought a new property from the Strozzi family at Poggio a Caiana north of Florence, to add to the already numerous country villas in Medici hands – Careggi, Cafaggiolo, Petraia, Fiesole and a number of places on the way to Pisa. The modest River Ombrone, once delightful and sparkling on its way across his new park not a hundred yards below the villa, is today a still, black strip of industrial liquid. Lorenzo's poem *Ambra* represents its river god as falling in love with a nymph when she takes a bathe naked. Today the river god is dead, and swimming in the river unthinkable. Yet this is no contradiction of Renaissance Florence, as guidebook thinking may suggest, but a development from it. Florence was pleasantly small for its power: the population was still not above a hundred thousand. It was a compact state: here lay its power to become the cradle of the modern world. And indeed the Medici family was the supreme pioneer of industrial society if ever there was one.

This was never a conscious aim among the first Medici. It was a logical conclusion of the financial power which Lorenzo was the first to feel, in a conflict that pervaded his life increasingly. Cosimo's favourite country seat, Careggi, was the opposite of grandiose. It belonged to the vine-yards and olive groves round it, and fitted snugly into them. It was the right place to die. And Lorenzo continued to go there for his family life. Clarice was a good wife, though she could hold nothing to the brilliant

OPPOSITE A retrospective portrait of Lorenzo by an artist of the later ducal Medici period, Giorgio Vasari (1511–71).

155

A letter from Lorenzo the Magnificent to the Prior of Siena, November 1487.

women of Florence – Cassandra Fidelis, the beautiful Alessandra della Scala (who once replied to a rejected lover in Greek) or Marietta Strozzi who was serenaded by a dozen or more gallants on a winter's night and then got into a snowball fight with them which she was allowed to win. Clarice was faithful, on the other hand, which few of the brilliant ones were. She produced good healthy children, and it looked as if the blight of gout would disappear (unfortunately with the brains) in the next generation. She played a definite role in Florentine life, and people came to her with petitions when they could not get direct access to her husband. Lorenzo enjoyed a simple family life. He romped with his children, sang and danced with them – which the splenetic Machiavelli, writing in the next century, thought lacking in self-respect. The children were numerous – Giuliano, Piero, Lucrezia, Giovanni, Maddalena, Luisa and Contessina. Piero was rather a handful. He was always in street brawls with other youths. There were one or two deaths 'in his presence', always hushed up, according to the later historian of Florence, Guicciardini. Luisa died while still engaged to a member of the junior branch of the Medici family, Giovanni. Lucrezia married Jacopo Salviati, later in a conspiracy to restore Lorenzo's son Piero after his banishment, thus reversing the treason of an earlier relative. Contessina married Piero Ridolfi, a son of the youth who had helped save Lorenzo's life in the cathedral.

In 1480 too, a new friend joined the group of thinkers and writers and artists round Lorenzo, those coddled and fussed-over men who could do no wrong in the Courts of the time, even when they had foul tempers and quarrelled like old women. The newcomer was altogether remarkable for looking and behaving like a gentleman and bringing a flood of new ideas which matured feverishly, perhaps too feverishly for his health, with every day that passed. This was Pico della Mirandola. His bearing was fine and upright. He had golden hair. He was remarkably eloquent, and had an astonishing memory. Here was the 'Renaissance man'. He had rank and wealth. He had studied law, which in those days meant that he could become a high-ranking official or the *Podestà*. He had been born at Mirandola in 1463, one of the younger sons of the prince of that place.

Pico della Mirandola, Marsilio Ficino and Agnolo Poliziano, the three principal neo-Platonists in Lorenzo's entourage, in a fresco by Cosimo Rosselli in the church of S. Ambrogio, Florence. Ficino started the informal 'Platonic academy' for Lorenzo's grandfather Cosimo, and translated Plato's works into Latin. All three thinkers were at some time followers of Savonarola.

He spent seven years wandering from one Italian university to another, and reached Rome when he was twenty-one with twenty-two different languages to his credit. Apparently, he needed to read or hear a poem only once to memorise it for life. In Rome he made the mistake of proposing for public debate nine hundred questions on every subject from mathematics to theology, and involving Hebrew, Arabic and Chaldean texts, all of which he had studied, together with the Cabbala. It was not the way to become popular in the Rome of Innocent VIII, and the Church began to examine his questions with inquisitorial eyes. They found thirteen of them heretical. He had to leave town in a hurry. This was what brought him to Florence and Lorenzo's willing protection. He subsequently (in 1486) wrote a treatise in Latin justifying his nine hundred questions in twenty days, and dedicated it to his new host. Agnolo Poliziano declared that there was something 'almost divine' in Pico's presence. No other city in the Italian peninsula was worthy of him.

He was an extreme neo-Platonist, and the other members of the Platonic academy round Lorenzo – Landino, Ficino and Poliziano – listened as if they had been waiting for him all these years. He wanted to find the unifying principle in all knowledge, all religion, even all superstition. Magic he saw as a force conferred on nature by God, and working through evil spirits. It is easy for us nowadays to see that his thought was shot through with eastern influences. And in so far as this was true, few people really understood him. He always called the East 'my own East'. He found in the Cabbala not only all Judaism but all Christianity. He wrote a book to prove that all learning lay in the history of the seven-day Creation. An immense number of schemes filled his mind to fever-point. He prepared a mystical commentary on Plato, a political history of divine doctrine, a 'harmony' of Aristotle and Plato, a polemic against the 'seven classes' of the enemies of the Church. He wanted to resolve all things into not a rational but a mystical order. As a child of the East, he refused to believe in disparate or disconnected knowledge on the obvious grounds that this denied the possibility of a spiritual origin. This led him to read far more than he could digest, in a well-nigh desperate effort to reach that divine cause which evaded all intellectual approach. He was always talking to Lorenzo and his friends about the 'dignity of man', meaning a supreme ethical destiny. In one respect, he had not absorbed the East – he argued that God had given man nothing of His own, though the power of attaining all. He did believe in free will. In this deep theological pessimism, combined with exultant confidence in grace-by-effort, he was perhaps more typical of the Renaissance than anyone else of the time.

In that Renaissance, there was always a strong sense of the need for a Reformation, and Pico della Mirandola was the first signal in Florence of that moral 'revival' which would bring the Medici state to the ground for a time and reduce Florence to a splendid backwater, its Medici – now

Grand Dukes – installed in the vast Palazzo Pitti. It was not enough for Pico to think and write. He behaved as he thought. He was almost a model for Florentine youth, though his reputation suffered a nasty fall in 1486 when he had an affair with someone else's wife in Arezzo (a Medici too). This lady, beautiful and rich, had previously been married to a trainer of horses for Florence's *palio*. She was now the wife of a poor member of the Medici House, a customs officer. It happened in May, a dangerous season for fine-looking young men and provincial heiresses. When Pico left town, she was seen riding pillion with him. The bells of Arezzo rang out and the local police gave chase. There was a fight outside the city, the lady was rudely dropped and several of Pico's men were killed. He got away but was arrested in the next village. Lorenzo got wind of the affair and had him released. As for the lady, she persuaded her husband that she had been walking outside the city gate, innocent as always, when this Pico della Mirandola whisked her up onto his horse and sped her away before she could say 'poor Medici'. He believed her, lacking her resources. As for the humanists in Florence, who could not make the story tally with their idea of Pico and the ethical dignity of man, they persuaded each other that, overwhelmed by his beauty, she had leapt on to Pico's horse of her own accord, and being ethically dignified he had not the heart to ask her to get off again. As for Lorenzo, he no doubt had a good laugh, being the most natural of the whole Platonic academy: Luigi Pulci probably spiced the story with his wit. The rest of Florence did not laugh. It could have said, with the Ferrarese ambassador, 'This unfortunate event is a subject of real regret, for apart from his learning he was regarded as a saint. Now, in this town, he has lost his character and his position, although similar mistakes have occurred to many men whom Venus has inflamed.'

Pico had for long been interested in Savonarola. This event drew him closer. Together with the poet Girolamo Benivieni, he became one of the priest's closest adherents. Benivieni turned his back on his Platonic past and warned people in his books that Plato's arguments must be discarded if they contradicted those of Aquinas, or went against the spirit of Christ. Florence had shown great daring, in thought and politics as in art: it had drawn conclusions from the famous ecumenical council in Cosimo's time which a good unadventurous priest might gib at. It had sailed perilously close to pagan Greek waters in an effort to open up Christian thought to a more inclusive summary of life. Christ and Plato had seemed all but merged for a time. The people had had nothing to do with this. They would not have understood the hour-long conversations about immortality which Lorenzo loved to have with his friends. They went to church and they said their 'Hail Maries'. More than this, the Church had a grip on men's minds which it is difficult for us to imagine today: the strength of that grip was basically medieval, offering hell-fire for disobedience and playing on those essentially pagan fears that never quite deserted the Italian imagination after the decadence of the Roman empire, when they had flourished to the point of hysteria. It was only a shameless man whose face did not twitch involuntarily with fear when a priest castigated. And when the priest spoke as movingly as Savonarola, one began to feel that one never wanted to think a free thought again, or paint a nude virgin again, or ask adventurous Platonic questions again, but hurry back to those dark, narrow arms in which at least one felt safe. Florence reacted quickly against its own period of experiment. It drew in its horns. That was what made Savonarola's book-burning possible after Lorenzo's death. It proved the Renaissance to be no rebirth at all, only the death of the Middle Ages, which meant the death of Church authority.

Pico burned all his love songs. He spent a fortune on the poor. He scourged himself. He even thought of becoming a friar, and at his death Savonarola put a Dominican habit on him. Savonarola killed Platonism, though in many ways his doctrines, especially that of 'the love of Jesus Christ', were Platonic in origin. He killed the Renaissance by persuading its protagonists to do the job for him. He brought down the Lorenzo régime because he understood its basic fallacy, that it unbalanced society by its banking principles, and its reliance on what the Church had once condemned as usury. If it spread through the world (which it did over the next four or five centuries), it would in the end produce a society obsessively engaged in a chase for wealth at the expense of even life itself. Through Savonarola, Lorenzo began to understand this too. But he could not undo what had become accepted practice. There were, after all, many other banking families which would have ruled Florence, and influenced Europe, far less well than he. The society which Savonarola produced in his short term of office was worse than the weakest Medici, including even Lorenzo's son Piero (banished after only two years of government), could have produced. But Savonarola would have replied to this that he was after souls, not savings.

Lorenzo too was after souls, in his very different way. Marsilio Ficino's neo-Platonic doctrine of 'purification by love', so close to Savonarola's, had released in Lorenzo his feeling for animals and nature. His descriptions of wood-life and the seasons are some of the most closely observed of his writing:

> *L'uliva, in qualche dolce piaggia aprica,*
> *Secondo il vento, par or verde, or bianca:*
> *Natura in questa tal serba, e nutrica,*
> *Quel verde, che nell' altre fronde manca . . .*

The olive tree, on some sweet open slope, appears now green, now white, according to the wind. In this, nature so stores and nurses the green that it is lacking in other bushes.

ABOVE This scene from the Otto Prints, a design for a toilet-case or work-box, shows a Florentine lady and gentleman of the fifteenth century walking with a musician. In the background are the Tuscan cypresses.

LEFT A gilded wooden mirror frame from the middle of the fifteenth century. It once belonged to the Medici family, and shows Venus, attended by putti and crowned with a garland, beside the sleeping Mars.

161

A self-portrait by Leone Battista Alberti (1404–72), the Florentine architect and theorist. Like Brunelleschi, Michelozzo, da Vinci and Michelangelo, he took ancient Rome as his model of 'harmony' in building. For Alberti the round form was the ideal.

It is a poem in the style of Ovid about winter at his newly-acquired villa, Poggio a Caiana. The Platonic influence makes him see everything as alive and connected, and from one divine emanation. Once, when he was nineteen, he had ridden out to the dense forests of Camaldoli near Arezzo for four summer days of discussion with his tutors Ficino and Landino, Leone Battista Alberti, architect and critic, and his thirteen-year-old brother Giuliano. These talks in the quiet of the hills, close to the Camaldoli abbey where they were lodging, were summarised by Landino in a book of dialogues called *Disputationes Camaldulenses*. On the first day, the question was raised, 'Which is better – the speculative or the active life?' Lorenzo came out on the side of the active life. That was where all his hopes, even his religious hopes, lay. It was what Savonarola never understood in him, and never tried to understand; Lorenzo wished to absorb the mystical realities into life, and make real things shine with their proper light which only ignorance made dark. This was why music was so important to him. It was 'divine sounds' reaching the heart. Ficino would come to his house with his fiddle, and Lorenzo stood Squarcialupi's uneven temper because he was the finest organist in Italy, if not Europe. Everything had to be drawn into the divine order, every superstition even, which meant ignorance too. This was why Pico della Mirandola found such a rapt audience at the house in Via Larga. Horoscopes, amulets (gems, lions' claws, adders' fangs) were all mixed in with Pythagorean numbers and harmonics. In Plato could be found Aristotle, Israel, Christ. In the end, there were no contradictions. In this yearning to reach what we would now call a global consciousness, and the divine principle in all religions, lay the courage of the humanist movement. In Florence and Lorenzo's circle it was foremost. Ficino strained to find Christ in Plato, comparing the Platonic 'souls of the spheres' with the angels, the 'punishment of the wicked' with hell, 'purification' with purgatory. As for Plato's doctrine of pre-existence and the transmigration of souls, it had to be covered up, since the boldest Christian mind at that time was not prepared to risk thinking about such a deeply Eastern and mystical analysis. But one could say that Pythagoras, Plato, the Jews and the pagans had all been struggling towards heaven in their way, and hoping for Christ. The humanists saw what the Church before and after them was not anxious to admit, that the Greek world had filtered through the Jewish world in the form of Christ's mission.

This informal Platonic 'academy' round Lorenzo was really the centre of Florentine life. Its members were called '*platonica familia*', and for each other they were '*frater in Platone*'. Ficino was the '*pater Platonicae familiae*'. Sometimes they met at the Badia in Fiesole, where Lorenzo had his precious library, and sometimes at Ficino's house nearby, a gift from Cosimo. At Lorenzo's suggestion, Plato's birthday was celebrated with a banquet. Nine guests were invited and the *Symposium* was read aloud, after which each guest made a commentary on it. A lamp was kept lit

before Plato's bust, and hymns were sung to him. Little wonder that Savonarola was itching to burn Lorenzo's library in the main square.

Luigi Pulci and Matteo Franco belonged to another side of Lorenzo's life: they shared his late nights and his women. Nannina, his sister, made many attempts to convert Luigi to a more thoughtful life, but he simply was not the type. Like Matteo, he had a keen wit, and could understand better than anyone Lorenzo's sharp switches from gaiety to sorrow, since that was how he felt too. Not that he was by any means the Court buffoon. In fact, Lorenzo used him constantly on diplomatic missions – to Milan, Venice, Bologna, Naples. When he died in 1484, Lorenzo felt that his house, and particularly his dinner table, was empty. Their friendship had dated from the time he had redeemed Luigi's small family estate in the Mugello for one of his brothers, Luca Pulci, who died in gaol and incidentally wrote a fine poem on Giuliano de' Medici's tournament, back in 1475.

Portraits of Matteo Franco and Luigi Pulci, close friends of Lorenzo, from a fresco in S. Trinità *c.* 1485, by Domenico Ghirlandaio. Franco and Pulci, both men of keen wit, shared Lorenzo's late nights. Pulci was unrepentantly ribald and his long mock-epic poem *Morgante* was among the books burned by Savonarola.

163

The Pulci were a family of poets. Luigi's famous *Morgante*, a long mock-epic poem, grew from the songs recited or sung at Lorenzo's dinner table. Everyone would invent new ridiculous situations for this story of giants. At that time, people were fascinated by combinations of tomfoolery and obscenity with high chivalrous romance. The *Morgante* stories became more and more extraordinary and hilarious. Considerations of geography were discarded as the struggles between the family Chiaramonte, the principle of good, and the family Maganza, the principle of evil, were waged over continents and oceans. Orlando and Rinaldo were the heroes. Margutte was the name of the lesser giant whose destiny it was to accompany the greater one, Morgante, the incarnation of mischief and self-seeking. Astarotte was the smart sceptic who never lacked a killing theological argument. Naturally, Pulci's work found its way onto Savonarola's pile, too.

Another detail from Ghirlandaio's S. Trinità fresco, showing Agnolo Poliziano and the young Giuliano de' Medici.

Pulci was both less learned and less religious than the rest of Lorenzo's circle. This was partly why Lorenzo loved him, needing an anchor in rough, natural talk of the kind his peasants would understand, to put against the artificiality that necessarily crept into Platonic discussions because ancient Greece was far away not only in time but in psychology. Luigi had refreshingly little sense, too, of the movement of moral re- vivalism which made his friends burn their books and pictures, and toss with remorse at night. Lorenzo loved a good laugh. In his sonnets, Luigi laughed at immortality and faith, though later he did recant. The family adored him and tenderly disapproved of him.

But closest of all to Lorenzo was Agnolo Poliziano, six years younger. His home town was Montepulciano, always noted for its blood feuds, one of which had involved his father, a lawyer called Benedetto Ambro- gini. At the time of Piero de' Medici's government, Benedetto was stabbed to death in his own home, and Agnolo, still a boy, was sent to Florence. There he studied under Marsilio Ficino, Cristofero Landini and the Greek Argyropoulos. There was little money in the family and he was haunted by the fear that he would one day have to stop studying, a fear which left him with a grasping disposition even when he was well established in Lorenzo's 'Court'. As a boy of seventeen, he had written to Lorenzo begging him for a robe and a pair of shoes. Lorenzo had probably heard something of him, since 'Poliziano' (a name he adapted from that of his birthplace) was already ardently interested in poetry. The story of his begging letter may be apocryphal, but the rest of it is that Lorenzo sent him at least two robes, and the boy wrote him such clever verses of thanks in reply that he took him into the Medici house- hold. The effect of his entry was much like that of Pico della Mirandola's a few years later: he was a shot in the arm for tired Platonists.

The most remarkable thing about Agnolo was that he thought and felt like the ancients, so deeply had he immersed himself in their work. Greek and Latin were spontaneous languages for him, which he spoke with the same ease as Italian, and perhaps with more. Of all the work written in Latin at that time, only his has survived, because it reads like an ancient author's. This is why classical scholarship in England calls him Politian and not Poliziano, as if he belonged to the authors of the empire. There was nothing he could not do in Latin. He wrote the tender, quite unmilitary *Giostra* for Giuliano's tournament. He wrote an elegy on the lovely Albiera degli Albizzi after her death. He translated the *Iliad*: Marsilio Ficino told him that no layman would be able to tell whether his Latin or the Homeric Greek was the original. He was interested in coins and inscriptions, and travelled everywhere in search of them. His was the first systematic study of these things as historical data. His *Nutricia* argued that poetry was the mother of civilisation, and it con- tained (this was typical of him) a critical list of the ancient poets. His lectures were never academic or dry. His *Ambra* praised Lorenzo's new villa as did Lorenzo's own poem of that name, but it was an introductory lecture to Horace, his first love among the Latin poets. His approach was full of surprises. He wrote a dramatic sketch called *Orfeo* in two days, in the Italian language amid Court festivities at Mantua. It was sung, not acted, and became the basis of the later opera. His epic for Giuliano's tournament never got to the subject of the joust itself, though this was its title: the first book praised the young Medici and his mistress, the second the House of the Medici, and there it stopped. Everyone marvelled at its subtle manipulation of language, the sense it gave of an inspired craftsman.

He was soon Lorenzo's closest friend, despite his unpleasant nature. Like the other Medici before him, Lorenzo could forgive anything of a brilliant and sincere man. Poliziano was always asking for favours and perquisites, not because he needed them but just in case his needs were forgotten. Under Lorenzo's influence he began writing ballads and short lyrics, some of which got out into the streets in carnival time. They were sung in Florence for generations afterwards. He became prior of San Paolo, and a canon of Florence's cathedral. He was not a religious man but the sermons of Fra' Mariano da Genazzano, a Franciscan monk with powers close to Savonarola's (though he was a kindlier, more tolerant man), moved him. Fra' Mariano had a dramatic effect on his congregation. He could move to pity, remorse or amusement in a moment. Poliziano cited him in his preface to his *Miscellanea* (addressed to Lorenzo) as a living refutation of the idea that ancient learning contradicted Christianity. In the same preface, he wrote that Florence had only four real critics, of whom Lorenzo and Pico della Mirandola were two. Since he himself was clearly the third, it left little room for the other humanists in town. It did not add to his popularity. When his great protector died, he was without a friend. Everyone from Savonarola downwards threw mud at him. He died a miserable death. He had recognised the craftsman in Fra' Mariano, not the saint. He paid for finding Savonarola uncouth.

Reading Poliziano, it would be difficult to see the struggles which were being played out at the time. In Lorenzo's work they are clear. In one of Lorenzo's youthful poems called *Altercazione*, he and a shepherd take it in turns to praise town and country, until Marsilio Ficino comes along with his lyre and tells them that happiness is found only in the spiritual life which raises men from earth to heaven. Lorenzo was not a reflective man like his grandfather, or a sedentary one like his father: in this the struggle to find spiritual soundness in an active life was all the greater. His writing was often close to Dante and Petrarch, especially in his sonnets, which he preferred to the rest of his work, and the *Silve d'Amore*, its main theme the death of his brother Giuliano's lover Simonetta Cattanei. But social activities kept breaking in, and his lyrical tone was touched with wry humour and scepticism. He wrote

OPPOSITE A page from a 1481 Florentine edition of Dante's *Divine Comedy*, with a Latin commentary by Cristofero Landino, one of Lorenzo's neo-Platonist teachers and friends. Twenty-four years older than Lorenzo, he also encouraged vernacular Italian, the language of Dante, Boccaccio and Petrarch.

to mouersi/se prima non si muoue la ragione . Entrai per lo camino alto:cioe profondo/chome diciamo
alto mare et alto fiume:perche el primo camino fu per linferno cioe per la cognitione de tutti: equali sono
infimi:perche sempre consistono circa le chose terrene . ET SILuestro:perche chome dicemo nel princi
pio epeccati nascono dalla selua cioe dalla materia che e/elcorpo .

CANTO TERTIO DELLA PRIMA CANTICA

P er me si ua nella citta dolente
  per me si ua nelletherno dolore
  per me si ua tra laperduta gente
Iustitia mosse el mio alto factore
  fecemi la diuina potestate
  la somma sapientia el primo amore
Dinanzi a me non fur chose create
  se non etherne et io etherno duro
  lasciate ogni speranza uoi chentrate
Queste parole di colore obscuro
  uidio scripte al sommo duna porta
  perchio maestro el senso lor me duro .

S ono alchuni equali credonoche edue primi capito
  li sieno stati inluoghi di proemio:et questo terzo
sia el principio della narratione . Ma se con'siderremo
chon diligentia tutta la materia/facilmente si puo pro
uare che la narratione comincia nel primo capitolo: et
nel uerso Io non ui so ben dire chomio uentrai . Impe
roche Danthe narra in questa sua peregrinatione esser
si ritrouato nella selua: et hauere smarrito la uia Essersi
condocto appie del monte . Et dipoi essersi addirizato
uerso el sole per erto camino elquale lo conduceua asal
uamento se le tre fiere non lauessino ripincto al basso.
Et finalmente ridocto quasi al fondo hauere hauuto el
soccorso di Virgilio et dalle tre donne . Et p lesue paro
le esser psuaso lasciado el corto ãdare del mõte seguitar
lo per linferno et purgatorio:laqual uia sanza sinistro
intoppo lo puo conducere al cielo . Ilche significa quel
lo che gia disopra habbiamo dimostro. Et se alchuno dicessi che in amendue questi canti molte chose scriue
conle quali capta beniuolētia et attētione et docilita: Enon si uieta che i ogni pte del poema non si possi fa
rr questo. Anzi maximamēte sirichiede allo scriptore che le capti douūque truoua occasione di poterlo fare
H'ora perche siamo gia al puncto chel poeta descende nellinferno . Giudico sia utile exprimere che chosa si
a inferno:et in quanti modi si dica alchuno scendere allinferno. Inferno adunque e/linfima: et bassa parte
del mondo/decto inferno da questa dictione infra che significa disocto:Ne solamente dal popolo di dio e/
posto lonferno: Ma anchora da molti poeti: et maxime da Homero da Virgilio. Ouidio. Statio: et Claudi
ano:Et molto piu egregiamente dal principe de philosophi Platone/Costui incritone nel qual libro induce
Socrate disputante della immortalita dellanimo/dimostra che lanime humane dopo la morte sono giudica
te secondo le loro colpe:et nellonferno tormentate insi no atanto che si purghino/se epeccati non sono sta
ti molto graui. Ma quelle che hanno commesso scelerateze enorme:et sono impurgabili secondo lui/sono
mandate in luogo piu profondo decto tartaro et quiui sono afflicte inetherno con grauissimi supplici. La
quale oppinione e/molto simile alla christiana fede:et abbraccia lonferno el purgatorio: Et la maggior pte

167

rispetti, those endless octaves which originated in Sicily or Naples, often improvised by the singer, in a show of ingenuity. *Rispetti* still go the rounds of a few dinner tables in Italy, each guest taking up a stanza in mounting complication and skill. In Lorenzo's *Necia da Barbarino*, the peasant Vallèra recites, with an ardour meant to be grotesque and therefore hilarious, the sacrifices he is going to make for his lover. His *Simposio* is a parody on the *Divine Comedy* in which he is taken by a friend, in a take-off of Dante's journey with Virgil, to see a cask of wine being broached at Ponte a Rifredi. Lorenzo had neither the time nor the solitude to make Dante's mystical journey himself. Yet he was aware of it. His life was in danger from assassins – and from the disease he inherited. He was inevitably the centre of bitter resentment and envy. There was little chance for him to rest. It was this that drew him towards extraordinary men. In the play he wrote for his children, called *San Giovanni e San Paolo* (the two eunuchs who suffered martyrdom under Julian the Apostate), Constantine – acted at home by himself – longs to give up 'the sweets of rule' which involve so much conflict for mind and body. He adds that a ruler, because he chastises other people's errors, must try to do no ill himself: his example is the key to his sway over the people. 'His eyes must always be open so that the others may sleep.' He was obliged to show courtesy and a sweet temper to everyone.

Only in riding and sitting at table with extraordinary men did Lorenzo find the release he needed. That was why no artist stayed long in Florence without getting some recognition from him, and why men of brilliant mind quickly found their way to his study.

Hardly an artist of the High Renaissance was not honoured or subsidised by the Medici family. Donatello, Castagno, Filippo Lippi, Fra' Angelico, Uccello, Benozzo Gozzoli, Ghiberti, Luca della Robbia, Desiderio da Settignano, Masolino, all flourished under Cosimo and Piero Only Masaccio, in some ways the father of fifteenth-century Florentine art, came before the Medicean period. Michelozzi, the architect of the earlier Medici country villas as well as of the house in Via Larga, accompanied Cosimo on his exile to Padua and Venice. Lorenzo inherited from his father Rossellino, Mino da Fiesole, the Pollaiuoli brothers and Verrocchio, together with the architects Giuliano da Sangallo and Benedetto da Mariano. He himself became the patron of Botticelli, Leonardo da Vinci, Ghirlandaio, Michelangelo, 'Cronaca', Lorenzo di Credi, Fra' Bartolomeo and Albertinelli, despite the fact that the plastic arts were not his first passion.

Florentine artists were employed on the Sistine chapel in Rome between 1480 and 1482. The ancient ruins they saw there for the first time stimulated a passion for architectural detail in painting: Botticelli, Ghirlandaio, Rosselli, Piero di Cosimo and Filippino Lippi all show this influence. It brought painting and architecture into close association. The entire house or church, from furnishings to proportions, was thought to

be in the field of the single artist. Botticelli painted banners and marriage chests. Pollaiuolo made inkstands and candlesticks. Hardly a painter did not at some time design a tapestry or a carpet. Thus the kind of collecting which Lorenzo did was not rich man's collecting as it came to be known in later centuries: first and foremost it was intended as a living example for local artists. When he bought fragments of ancient Roman statuary or an ancient medallion, it was not primarily to embellish his home, as many historians following the Savonarolist and Machiavellian line have maintained, but to give men like Michelangelo their models. If the sculptured forms in the Etruscan-Roman tomb of the Volumnius family outside Perugia can hardly be distinguished in style from Michelangelo's forms in the Medici chapel at San Lorenzo, it is for this reason. Lorenzo was not simply a patron in the modern sense, dispensing meals and clothes and commissions. He was a teacher. This was why he took the boy Michelangelo to see his collection on free afternoons.

His favourite artists were Verrocchio, Botticelli and Ghirlandaio – the craftsman, the neo-Platonist and the narrator. He had no great patience where art was concerned. He looked for striking and finished qualities, and Leonardo da Vinci found his fame and his chances in Milan because during Lorenzo's period he was still in an experimental mood. Perugino, too – though Lorenzo received him into his house and gave him a salary and commissions – had something strangely at variance with the

A bronze relief showing a battle between Romans and barbarians by Bertoldo di Giovanni (*c.* 1420–91), a pupil of Donatello, chosen by Lorenzo de' Medici to run the 'school' of artists in his household (including the young Michelangelo). This piece shows the influence of ancient Roman sarcophagi.

Michelangelo's *Battle of the Centaurs* executed in 1492, the year of Lorenzo de' Medici's death. It is an early work, in marble, and was inspired by an ancient relief, no doubt one that had been brought to Florence from Rome by one of the artists in Lorenzo's 'Court'. Michelangelo was a young protégé of Lorenzo's.

other artists of the time: his scenes were bathed in a mellow light that seemed to fall on them like dust, but it was a mystical dust, not declared in bold, dramatic, immediate terms that the eye could decipher easily. He too found his fame elsewhere – at the Court of Milan, where he went on Lorenzo's recommendation. He was never part of Lorenzo's Court like Botticelli or even the young Michelangelo. For in Florence art and social life were closely connected and it seemed natural that the 'best' artists should be close to the man who ruled the city. The danger was that the work of even these marvellous artists should become something like commodity-art, and basically decorative. Michelangelo blinded Italy with his power: like Beethoven in music, he could be described as the bombshell that ended Italian art. In his name, frescoes of an earlier era were whitewashed or painted over. Luckily for us, many towns were not rich enough to commission new works in the post-Michelangelo epochs, and we can still see frescoes by Simone Martini, Lorenzetti, Bartolo di Fredi, Barna da Siena. In the light of these works, much of what was done in the High Renaissance, even much of Michelangelo, may seem too complete (is this why Michelangelo's unfinished *Pietà* is so much admired?). Money-operations and art were not simply closely connected in the Medici era, they complemented and supported each other. The Medici and other families sent to the Netherlands for pictures by Jan van Eyck, Pieter Christophsen and Memling. Such a passion for collecting did not begin with the desire to embellish, but the more money the family had, the more art began to serve a consumer principle. Only in the Sienese school and in the early Florentines, such as Giotto and Cimabue and Masaccio, is this quite absent. The process had not by that time got under way.

A fifteenth-century illustration of a bear hunt from the Otto Prints series, from a set of designs for the cover of a wooden box.

Seven Saints by Fra' Filippo Lippi, once an overdoor in the Palazzo Medici. The saints depicted seem to be connected with the descendants of Giovanni di Bicci de' Medici. The central figure is St John the Baptist for Giovanni himself.

Verrocchio became a fashion. He had learned sculpture under Donatello, and worked with him at San Lorenzo; Filippo Lippi influenced his painting. Verrocchio did portrait busts in terra cotta (both Lorenzo and Giuliano sat for him). After the Pazzi conspiracy, three wax figures were modelled from Verrocchio's drawings of Lorenzo. He brought in the vogue of the death-mask, and to him we owe that of Lorenzo. But he was more than a fashion, he was a great teacher too. He influenced widely different artists such as Leonardo da Vinci and Lorenzo di Credi, and Botticelli and Perugino. Di Credi and Leonardo worked in his studio. But here too the influence tended towards the commodity

principle, which is partly what Vasari meant when he said that Lorenzo di Credi was too neat (no dust was allowed in his studio in case it spoiled the surfaces) and too minutely careful.

Botticelli was in every way Lorenzo's 'Court painter'. He too did portraits. There is one at Chantilly of the lovely Simonetta Cattanei. In his *Adoration of the Magi* at the Ufizzi, there are portraits of Cosimo, Lorenzo and Giuliano, together with Poliziano, Strozzi and the painter himself. Both his *Birth of Venus* and his *Primavera* were painted for Lorenzo. So was his *Pallas Athene*, a favourite subject of Lorenzo's. He was given the job of painting a great fresco of the Pazzi conspiracy on the

outside wall of the Signoria which has since been worn away by time. For a cousin of Lorenzo's, he did the famous *Dante* drawings, ninety of them in all. Filippo Lippi was the principle influence on his work, together with Ghirlandaio: Lippi's favourite red and white roses figure often in his work, and his *Magi* was for a long time taken for Ghirlandaio's. But there was something in Botticelli which no artist had before or since, and which singled him out from all the Renaissance artists: he was the one consciously and even yearningly neo-Platonist artist. It gave his main work a literary quality – some would say artificial. His colours are rarified. His figures float. But it is much more than a fairy-tale. It is the story of the human creature as a god. The feeling is not mystical as in Perugino, or sweetly religious as in the earlier artists such as Simone Martini and Lorenzetti. There is a new feeling. It came from the ardent discussions that went on in the Lorenzo group. It grew also from Lorenzo's company. They were pagans together, before heavy responsibilities fell on Lorenzo. They roamed the streets and, together with Pulci, found the same women. Botticelli tried to capture a new joy which was for long misunderstood – until the revival of his fame in the nineteenth century, mainly through English collectors. He was always original. Every gesture in his paintings had a meaning (the precise meaning of *Primavera* is still not certain). He was the closest of the artists to the poets – Poliziano especially. In this he resembles Perugino more than any Florentine, in his effort towards poetry, leaving both narrative and naturalism behind. Some said that he always painted the same woman, whether it was a Madonna or Venus. His *Adoration of the Magi*, being narrative and close to Ghirlandaio, was not at all typical of him. Like Pico della Mirandola and Marsilio Ficino he was looking for a certain enchanted stillness, the food of all religious experience, the common principle of all theologies. Like Pico, he suddenly took fright, succumbing to that remorse and self-castigation which had been so deep in Christian attitudes since the time of the desert fathers. Original sin closed its dark hand over his work, and he became one of the most ardent Savonarolists in Florence. After that, he wanted to do nothing but Madonnas and Nativities. The earlier joy capsized into something more durable, but narrow too. Here can be read the failure of the Renaissance as in almost no other artist, for no other artist tried so hard to break down the narrative form, and achieve a new Greece, not simply a repetition of Greek figures and faces.

He was not an interesting colourist. The line and the movement take precedence over colour, so much that his pictures have been classed as 'tinted line'. He tended to be careless in his backgrounds: the detailed background in his work at the Sistine chapel is said to have been done by his pupil Filippino Lippi. But in this almost deliberate retraction from vivid materials, he was close to Lorenzo: he was the poet's painter. His work posed no artistic problems. Unlike Michelangelo, he did not seem

OPPOSITE A self-portrait by Sandro Botticelli from his painting *The Adoration of the Magi*. Botticelli was one of Lorenzo's closest friends. The most neo-Platonic of Florence's artists, he became an ardent Savonarolist and disclaimed the earlier work for which he is now famous.

OPPOSITE A Florentine jar from around 1460.

BELOW A cup of pink Sicilian jasper on a silver gilt base, formerly in Lorenzo's private collection, sacked after his death by French troops. LAV are the first letters of LAVR MED, denoting that it was a commission from the Medici family.

to be working for the future. In that too he was pleasing to Lorenzo: his works gratified in a simple and direct way, without intricate layers of paint and clever brushwork, and yet they provoked the kind of thinking that was like air to men such as Poliziano and Ficino. It was an attempt to catch spirituality without much mystical experience. This Botticelli himself felt when he became perhaps the most ardent Savonarolist in Lorenzo's circle. Other artists who worshipped the preacher were Piero di Cosimo, Lorenzo di Credi, 'Cronaca', and, among the younger students, Fra' Bartolomeo and Michelangelo. The feeling was that there had been too much experiment, too much daring. Suddenly the courage collapsed. The artist turned on himself, his past. He paid the price for being socially too well received. Lorenzo di Credi, too, burned a great deal of his work. And later all of Florence felt the same timidity, as if it had stretched itself in ideas and ambitions far beyond its powers. After Lorenzo's son, there was no more republic and no more real independence.

ABOVE The courtyard of the
Badia in Fiesole. Here or at the
nearby villa belonging to
Ficino, Lorenzo would spend
hours in discussion with other
members of the informal
Platonic Academy.

OPPOSITE A page from
Marsilio Ficino's translation
from Plotinus. Inside the M in
the first line is a portrait of
Ficino.

The painter Piero di Cosimo expressed this remorse and anguish
throughout his life. He was never in Lorenzo's Court, though he was
close to Botticelli in style. In fact, he was a recluse, and people considered
him weird. Of all the Florentine artists, he was perhaps the nearest to
Venice's Giorgione, not in the way in which he used paint, but in his
strangely elusive symbolism. He hated neatness. No plant in his garden
must be pruned. There was never a broom in his studio. He found
the crying of children unbearable – coughing men as well, and friars,
and churchbells. Like Filippo Maria Visconti, the late Duke of Milan, he
was terrified of thunderstorms and would crouch in a corner wrapped in
his cloak. When he was working hard on an effect, he would boil fifty

PROHEMIVM MARSILII FICINI FLOREN
TINI IN LIBROS PLOTINI AD MAGNA
NIMVM LAVRENTIVM MEDICEM
PATRIAE SERVATOREM I

MAGNVS COSMVS

An illuminated *Book of Hours* belonging to Lorenzo de' Medici and dated 1485. The miniatures, showing the Annunciation and Virgin and Child, are by Francesco d'Antonio del Chierico.

VITA PLOTI
NIETEIVS.
LIBRI·LIIII·A
MARSILIO
FICINO·TRA
DVCTIET·EX
POSITI·AD
MAGNANI
MVM·LAV
RENTIVM
MEDICEM
PATRIAE
SERVATOREM

eggs at a time while making his size, and eat his way through them over the next few days. But even he had his fashionable hour. It was impossible in Lorenzo's Florence to be gifted and unrecognised.

Domenico Ghirlandaio was almost exactly contemporary with Lorenzo. He was of all Florence's artists the most like a man of commerce. He never refused a commission and not even Lorenzo's patronage could contain his hunger for work. He painted for the Tornabuoni in both Florence and Rome, and for the Lyons bankers Sassetti. And of all Florence's artists, he looked least beyond the present order of things. He painted with narrative fidelity. The splendour of the human face, of textures and backgrounds, was enough for him. He was for this reason never close to Lorenzo as was Botticelli. His life was the workshop, and while this excited Lorenzo's awe, it did not move him as Botticelli's bubbling, sympathetic nature did. The Santa Maria Novella series of frescoes shows the lives of the Madonna and John the Baptist in terms of the Tornabuoni household, its births and weddings and banquets. In one of the groups stand Marsilio Ficino, Cristofero Landino, Agnolo Poliziano and Gentile Becchi. He painted the people he saw. He was not torn this way and that. Therefore his work has a remarkable straightness and sanity, a record of created marvels. His St Francis cycle at the church of Santa Trinità shows Maso degli Albizzi, Agnolo Acciaiuolo, Palla Strozzi and Lorenzo himself.

In Florence, art did not occupy an area of amusement or decoration, separate from the rest of life. Lorenzo's 'patronage' was a full-time activity, and other princes such as King Ferrante and Ludovico *il Moro* in Milan were constantly writing to him for a musician or painter or man of learning. He felt it as much his work to supply them with what they wanted as to send them a diplomat loaded with political arguments. For diplomacy he often used the brilliant Braccio Ugolino. But Ugolino could do much more than argue a point. When he came to Lorenzo's house he brought his fiddle with him and a group of servants to sing. There were five organs in the Medici palace. Musicians came to Lorenzo from the famous Belgian school – Josquin des Près of Hainault, Agricola and Obrecht (who taught Erasmus music). Heinrich Isaak from Bohemia was for several years in his service. He set Lorenzo's one drama to music and most of his ballads and part-songs for the carnivals. He adored Florence, found it the 'worthiest, the most beautiful city' he knew. He too was influenced towards the popular by Lorenzo, having until then, like most of the Netherlands composers, written only sacred music.

It was not that the Medici household sang and played and talked Plato into the night and gazed at new pictures from Flanders as a rest from party politics and money. The activities were one and the same. Only Lorenzo's political enemies spread the legend, with the help of an unforgiving Church, that he used the one to cover the other. He needed the art even more than the money.

OPPOSITE The dedication page (*'ad magnanimum Laurentium Medicem'*) from Marsilio Ficino's translation of the Alexandrian thinker Plotinus, whose ideas were basic to the Florentine Platonic Academy.

Part Five

The Last Years

Lorenzo had defied the King of Naples at Piombino, the Pope at Imola, and he had paid a handsome price. The Pope had crudely wanted to eliminate him, the King of Naples more wisely to bring him to heel. King Ferrante's policy was the more successful of the two. After the disastrous war, Lorenzo learned to approach powerful princes, and this included the Prince of the Church, with caution and reserve. He learned that it was worthwhile to work hard for peace in the Italian peninsula rather than for short-term advantages like the possession of a small Mediterranean port. As for the Pazzi conspiracy, that had simply been part of a concerted plan to get rid of him, and finally had little to do with the Pazzi family itself. He could say this: the struggle with the Pazzi had paid off. He had no powerful banking rivals in the field. The Medici family name was interchangeable with that of Florence in all the Courts of Europe.

He set about making that position all the firmer. There would be no more successful conspiracies. But he did not produce a personal tyranny. Medici government was never, in any case, personal government, as its political enemies of the time tried to make it seem. It was party government. And what Lorenzo and his closest advisers now did was to build a new constitution round the party. If you had nothing Medicean about you, you could not get your nose into the Signoria.

The usual juggling with numbers started all over again. The Signoria was authorised to elect thirty men, and to nominate 210 men qualified for state office and free of state debt, their age at least thirty. Together with the thirty, the Signoria, the Colleges and this new council were to scrutinise all the names due to be placed in the boxes for drawing when the time came to select state officials. For this job they were to associate themselves with a further body of forty-eight men. It was a way of screening every political man in the city. An electoral body of 362 men controlled the offices of state for the whole population.

To ensure that no family (this really meant no family other than the Medici) should exercise undue influence on this body, it was laid down that no more than three members of any family might join the 210 or the Thirty. While the constitution was still being rigged, the Signoria and the Colleges, together with the 210 and the Thirty, formed a council of reform. They revised the state debt, raised taxes to meet the interest on it and underwrote schemes for the relief of the country districts ruined by the recent war.

On 16 April 1480, the Signoria came up with yet another number.

This was the Council of Seventy. First of all, thirty were to be nominated by the Signoria, and these elected the remaining forty. Really it was a senate, on the Venetian model, and an essential link between the executive and the legislative arms. Each of the Forty had to be at least forty years old. Three quarters of them had to come from the major guilds. Above all, the members of the Seventy sat for life. It ensured experience

The neo-Platonic sense of beauty which Michelangelo had first met in the circle of Lorenzo the Magnificent found its full expression in the monument to Lorenzo's grandson, the Duke of Urbino.

and quick action in an emergency. The Seventy were responsible for electing the chief justices, and took the place of the *accopiatori*, the board of selection which had hitherto given the leading party control of the Signoria. It elected from itself eight men who supervised all aspects of state and foreign policy. And it elected twelve who looked after the state debt, the Admiralty and the Board of Trade. It was efficient government for the first time.

In the Eight and the Twelve there was a hint of an over-concentration

ABOVE The thirteenth-century courtyard of the palace of the Podestà in Florence. It is decorated with Florentine coats-of-arms.

BELOW An engraving showing Renaissance methods of torture, commonly applied to both military prisoners and suspected criminals to extract information or confessions.

of power, so, like Venice's Ten, they were limited to a period of office of six months. They were an ideal instrument for a well-organised party to use. People thought it looked like personal tyranny only because Lorenzo was an excellent party chief. After all, he had been at the game since early youth.

And then the constitutional change was a security measure. The party consolidated its forces against the chance of another conspiracy, or another war. Nerves were still raw. In September 1480 a pilgrim called at the Medici villa at Poggio a Caiano and asked for shelter. The servants took him for an assassin. He was taken to the Bargello and put to atrocious tortures – including the roasting of the soles of his feet from which he died, and no one could say whether he was an assassin or not.

In the spring of the following year, there was another serious attempt on Lorenzo's life. Like all the other plots against his person, it emanated from the ubiquitous and determined nephew of the Pope, Girolamo Riario. Three men, all of them from good and prominent families (only one of them Florentine), were involved in a conspiracy to do what the Pazzi had failed to do. One of them, Mariotto Baldovinetti, lived in Rome and was thought to be Riario's agent. The second, Battista Frescobaldi, had been resident in Peru. One of the Pazzi conspirators, Baroncelli, had ended up there and Frescobaldo had helped extradite him. He felt that he had been improperly rewarded for this. He and Baldovinetti conceived the plot together in Rome. The third, Francesco Balducci, was the Florentine involved, and the only one of the three to escape (his brother was hanged in his stead). All three men had bad reputations.

The plan was to assassinate Lorenzo during Whitsuntide and once more invite the people to revolution. In the poor quarters of the city, barrels of wine were to be placed in certain doorways to help the revolutionary idea. It was a far more wretched thing than the Pazzi conspiracy, since the men involved had no hope of arousing sympathy among Florentines, rich or poor, and there was no army, let alone a pope, to back them up.

Preparations for the murder never started because the plot was exposed too soon: this meant that it was difficult for the Signoria to put the men to death, their crime being only a verbal one. But conspiring 'against liberty', even verbally, was taken as high treason, and they were hanged.

But hanging conspirators did not advance the city's finances, which were in a sorry state. Lorenzo and his financial advisers set about trying to get Florence on its feet again by drawing ashore the state galleys which had monopolised all of Florence's trade with the Levant, so that any merchant who wished could ship his goods direct. Trade negotiations were started with Egypt. A new free trade policy meant that cheap woollens came in from Lombardy and England, which eased the hardship among working people.

An early sixteenth-century Swiss woodcut. Hanging was the most common form of capital punishment in the Renaissance.

Eclipse

A woodcut of Florence, dated about 1486. The Badia Fiesolana, where Lorenzo and his friends spent many hours in Platonic discussion, is shown on its hill outside the city, towards the right.

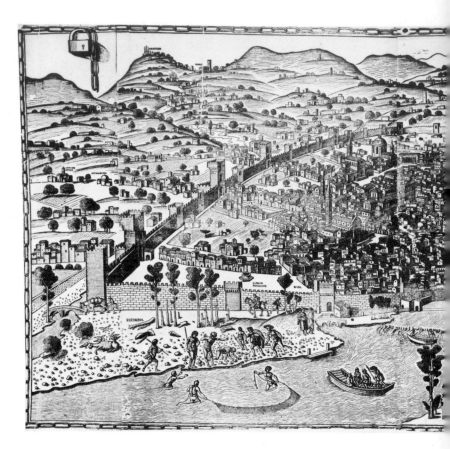

The Turks had saved Lorenzo, but the whole of Europe was in danger from them. The death of Mohammed II on 3 May 1481 removed the danger: his heir, Bajazet, was in dispute with his brother Djem, and in any case was much less expansionist than his father. He was also less efficient. The garrison at Otranto was abandoned by the autumn, and the Duke of Calabria took the credit for having recaptured the town. Many of the Turks taken prisoner entered service with Naples, a valuable contribution for Ferrante as they were better engineers than Christians. It seemed the right time for a Crusade, and Ferrante tried to persuade the Pope to organise one. But Crusades were hardly in fashion then: princes were too busy building their own power. Girolamo Riario was also against it. He took Forlì instead. Antoniello Ordelaffi, a member of

Forli's traditional ruling family, had seized the government of the city, which gave Girolamo the excuse to drive him out and re-establish the government in the name of the former ruler's infant son, who in turn handed the state over to Girolamo. It was easier than fighting Turks.

Every day it was clearer to Lorenzo that the Pope's nephew might prove more dangerous than Turks and Pope together. He was getting dangerously near Florence's trade outlets. It looked as if Faenza would be the next to go. If that was the case, Florence would be sealed off from the Adriatic. He promptly offered help to Antoniello Ordelaffi and sent envoys to the Manfredi who controlled Faenza. Ordelaffi with his men raided the road between Forli and Imola (also in papal hands) so as to make communication between the two impossible.

A marble portrait-relief of
Ercole d'Este (1431–1505),
Duke of Ferrara.

Bigger game than Faenza interested Girolamo. This was Ferrara in the
north, an excellent springboard for possible attacks west on Milan and
south on Tuscany. He made a deal with Venice, which received him like
a prince. It was agreed that Venice would take certain territories round
Ferrara on which there were imperial fiefs, while the Pope took Ferrara
itself. As for Girolamo's dashing about all over Italy, that was all right by
Venice (and he might even subdue Naples). Venice then picked a quarrel
with Ferrara. The Serenissima had the right to maintain a resident judge
in that city to deal with lawsuits involving Venetians. This judge had

recently been excommunicated by the Bishop of Ferrara's vicar for certain dealings he had had with a priest tried for debt. Venice asked, as a concession to smooth over this little quarrel, that she be given the monopoly in salt manufacture for the entire north of Italy. It was really asking the Duke of Ferrara to give up manufacturing salt at Comacchio, and this he refused to do, as Venice knew he would. War was declared on him in May 1482.

Lorenzo was watching hard – not that he was in as tight a corner as before – Ludovico *il Moro* would enter the field with him, in his own interests. Naples was none too pleased at a Venice–Rome axis. Genoa (hostile to Milan) and Siena (hostile to Florence) would naturally be on the Pope's side. Mercenary captains everywhere began to look happy again, now that the chances of a general Italian peace looked slim. Venice persuaded the Duke of Savoy and the Marquis of Montferrat to come in against Milan. She also put Ruberto Malatesta on contract, while Milan signed up Federigo of Urbino. The leadership of the Florentine army went to Costanzo Sforza. Ruberto San Severino, one of the previous claimants to the Milanese throne, had fled to Venice after quarrelling with Ludovico *il Moro* on the grounds that the young Duke of Milan was not given enough say in the state's affairs. It looked as if Girolamo Riario had manœuvred Milan and Venice into a first-class war.

Meanwhile, Lorenzo set out to harry the Pope on his northern frontiers. The Manfredi of Faenza and the Ordelaffi of Forlì were to harry Girolamo in the Romagna. Niccolò Vitelli once more chased papal troops out of Città di Castello and reinstated himself there. The road between Rome and Tuscany was now blocked.

San Severino crossed the Adige and took Ficarolo. But by this time Naples and the Colonna family in Rome had joined forces, and the Duke of Calabria with Colonna got as far as the walls of Rome, ravaging wherever they went. The Pope sent wild appeals to Venice to send him Malatesta, whose timely arrival saved him. The Neapolitans retreated south to Santa Maria in Formis, not the place to be in the summer because of its mosquitoes. Malatesta pressed on and pushed them even further to Sermoneta. Here the Turkish prisoners in his pay saved the Duke of Calabria's life, by holding the retreat with suicidal courage. Instead of going on to Naples, Malatesta followed the mercenary rule and returned to Rome in triumph. There he died. Some say that he drank the water of Santa Maria in Formis during the heat, and died of a fever, others that he was poisoned by Girolamo for not finishing his job.

The war was not going dangerously for Florence, but Lorenzo had learned how suddenly fortunes could change when there were armies in the field. He worked hard to bring the Pope to peace, knowing too that Girolamo Riario's rash influence was waning at the Vatican. Sixtus had got his fingers burned. There was little point in provoking all of Italy and the rest of Europe too – as a new influence at the Vatican, Giuliano della Rovere (later Julius II), another nephew, pointed out. He had never liked this war. And he did not share the Pope's hatred of the Medici. He could also read the true meaning of the recent treaty with Venice better than the violent and unreasoning Girolamo. He saw that Venice would scoop up Ferrara, since that town was on her doorstep. And this would give her a springboard for later attacks into papal Romagna. Even Sixtus saw the force of della Rovere's arguments. Hitherto he had seen Lorenzo as the chief obstacle before his own expansion in the north. Now he was persuaded that it was Venice.

The peace which in fact ensued was very much Lorenzo's quiet work, though it was the immediate achievement of the Spanish ambassador at Rome. By now, Ferdinand and Isabella of Spain were alarmed at the state of Italy, especially when the Pope invited the Dauphin of France to bring an army down. Giuliano della Rovere was proved right: Venice refused to give up Ferrara. The allies, as they now were (Naples, Milan, Ferrara and Mantua), met together at Cremona to decide what should be done. Lorenzo represented Florence at the talks, despite a letter from Louis XI warning him not to take long journeys for fear of Girolamo Riario's knife. But he went, and his arguments carried the day.

It was decided that the allies would take the offensive. It was to be a new war. Venetian territory would be partitioned. Ferrante insisted that Ravenna and Cervia should go to Girolamo Riario, Brescia and Bergamo to Milan, while Florence and Naples were to get nothing. The Florentine general Costanzo Sforza refused to go on fighting at Ferrara, perhaps in collusion with Venice, and Florence's Eight of War dismissed him.

Lorenzo now turned his diplomatic gifts to harrying Venice. He received a Turkish ambassador in Florence, which caused a certain panic in the Doge's palace – Turks at sea and mercenary armies on land were more than Venice could take. In desperation, she encouraged the Duke of Orleans to press his claim to Milan, and Louis XI to give his support to the Duke of Lorraine in his claim to Naples. This time the 'allies' were a little shaken, and it looked as if peace was needed on both sides. The treaty – signed at Bagnolo in August 1484 – was mostly Ludovico *il Moro*'s work. He had most to fear from France, after all. Nor was he too happy at the Duke of Calabria's presence in Lombardy. Some say that he was sweetened by Venetian diplomats to the tune of 60,000 ducats. The other 'allies' were none too happy, but a bad peace was better than war.

Venice agreed to give up the towns which she had seized along the Apulian coast. The River Po was to become her southern frontier. In other words, Girolamo Riario had stirred Italy up to less than no purpose, since the Pope was the major loser. News of the bad peace killed Pope Sixtus. He went into a rage that silenced and immobilised him for thirty hours together and then he died on 12 August 1484. People said that as he

had lived by war, it was natural that peace should be his death.

Lorenzo had laid hold of the town of Citerna near Arezzo, but he gave it up to Ferdinand and Isabella of Spain. He acted as intermediary between Niccolò Vitelli and the Pope. Vitelli recognised papal suzerainty but was for all practical purposes in Lorenzo's pocket. Rimini stayed with Malatesta's bastard. Lorenzo had even maintained good relations with Siena, mostly by not harrying her possessions. He had an agent watching events in that city from a nearby castle. This Piero Giovanni Ricasoli reported to him that the Sienese were a bunch of fools and would make twenty-five revolutions in a day for a drink. Naturally, Lorenzo could afford the drink. A small revolutionary group of thirty men gathered in the city's piazza and an unpopular magistrate was thrown to the pavement from the windows of Siena's Signoria. More rebels joined the party in the square, and more magistrates were flung from the windows. The new government was little more than Lorenzo's puppet. He had come off quite well from *this* war.

Siena, a view of the city from the cathedral tower, showing the famous Piazza del Campo immediately below. A strong financial power in the Middle Ages, Siena was always happy to weaken Florence whenever the chance occurred, and throughout the Medici republic she launched constant raids into Florentine territory. Towards the end of Lorenzo's life the city became a Florentine puppet.

OPPOSITE A portrait of
Savonarola by Fra' Bartolomeo
(1475–1517). The Dominican
preacher, famous in Florence
for his castigations of the rich
and his direct, fervent
language, came from Ferrara.
After four years of supremacy
in Florence he was tried and
burned in 1498.
OVERLEAF Botticelli's
Adoration of the Magi with
portraits of the Medici
dynasty.
BELOW Lucca's imposing
twelfth-century cathedral.

He had also found a chance, in the general mêlée, of getting back some essential places he had lost. A Florentine convoy to the castle of Sarzanella, which overlooked the much coveted town of Sarzana, was attacked by a small Genoese force. The castle was Florentine. It gave Lorenzo the excuse he needed. He sent a mercenary army under three commissioners, Jacopo Guicciardini, Bongianni Gianfigliazzi and Antonio Pucci, to attack Pietrasanta, from which the Genoese had launched their attack. Antonio Pucci went round the camp with gold and for once mercenaries decided to win a battle. Pietrasanta was now in Lorenzo's hands. This was as useful as Sarzana had been to block the road from the north. It had another use: it put Lucca at Lorenzo's mercy. Lucca had built Pietrasanta as its trade outlet to the Riviera coast.

HIERONYMI·FERRARIENSIS·A·DEO·
MISSI·PROPHETÆ·EFFIGIES·

With care, never venturing his neck too far, Lorenzo had got back Florence's old position. Tuscany was safe for her trade. Both coasts lay open to her trains. He was once more in close friendship with Milan. Above all there was a new Pope (Innocent VIII) who was so indebted to Giuliano della Rovere for having rigged his election with money and promises that he left most of his political decisions to him. Guidantonio Vespucci wrote to Lorenzo on the subject of this new pope, excusing himself for the lateness of his letter as 'Antonio Tornabuoni sent off his despatches without waiting for mine, I being at Mass with other ambassadors.' He had found Innocent most kindly and sympathetic as a cardinal: 'he used to embrace everyone, and kiss some more than you can imagine'. Innocent lacked experience of state affairs and was not very learned, but for all that was not exactly ignorant. He had an open face and was well-built. He was about fifty-five years old. He had a brother and a good many bastard children, at least one male, and some daughters already married. He had revealed himself to be a man more for taking advice than giving it.

It was a great chance for Lorenzo to heal his relations with Rome once and for all. Girolamo Riario looked as if he were no longer a potential

A bird's-eye view of Tuscany by Leonardo da Vinci showing Pisa and Volterra.

OPPOSITE Pope Leo X (Lorenzo de' Medici's second son Giovanni), Pope from 1513 to 1521, with the cardinals Giulio de' Medici and Luigi de' Rossi, by Raphael (1483–1526). Giovanni was the first Medici to be Pope, and his election was the result of prolonged effort on his father Lorenzo's part.

victor, and Lorenzo's private agents tried now and then to hasten his departure with the help of a knife. Girolamo threatened to burn down Giuliano della Rovere's house in Rome, but the threat came to nothing. Lorenzo sent his eldest son, Piero, now fourteen years old, to congratulate the new Pope on his accession, just as his father had sent him years before on a similar mission. The difference was that Piero lacked his powers – particularly personal magnetism and judgment. Piero was briefed to recommend his brother Giovanni for a cardinal's hat. He was accompanied by Bartolomeo della Scala, Florence's chancellor, and Agnolo Poliziano (who, having quarrelled with Clarice over the education of Lorenzo's children, was only too happy to get away). Lorenzo wrote Piero a letter advising him to behave naturally and not to show off his learning or use impolite expressions: 'Wherever you find yourself with other young people belonging to missions bear yourself seriously and respectfully, and with humanity towards your equals, taking care with those older than yourself not to take precedence, because being my son you are nothing more than a citizen of Florence.'

But there were new troubles, arising from Giuliano della Rovere's preference for France over Spain. He had thwarted the election of the Cardinal of Aragon to the papal chair. He had also encouraged Innocent to extract his full tribute from Naples instead of the white palfrey which Sixtus had agreed to receive in its stead. It was not long before there was war between Naples and Rome, especially after Ferrante seized the persons of a number of barons on the papal-Neapolitan border, among them the Count of Montorio.

Hitherto Ferrante had been tolerant of these wild men who acknowledged no one's rule but their own. Now he gave more ear to his son, the Duke of Calabria, whose answer as always was brutality and over-taxation. The noblemen of Aquila murdered the royal governor and his Neapolitan garrison. Ferrante sent an army north which would have entered Rome without difficulty had it not been for the arrival of Ruberto San Severino, whom Venice had sent down to help the Pope. Lorenzo had to walk the tightrope between two warring sides as never before in his career. There was a complicating factor in Florence's personal hatred of the Duke of Calabria, which Lorenzo must try not to give way to. It still rankled in the heart of the people that this rascal, on his recent visit to the city, when coming south from his Lombardy campaign, had refused to descend from his horse, like Federigo years before.

Lorenzo was able to prevent the Sienese from going over to the papal side, though hardly a year before they had all but become the willing tools of the Duke of Calabria. This was for the very good reason that the nobles financed and encouraged by the Duke were no longer in power, and the city feared the Duke's retaliation if he beat the Pope.

Innocent repeated Sixtus's last-ditch threat, to call down the French

OPPOSITE A view of Siena, from the town hall, showing the cathedral on the left.

on Naples in a revival of the Angevin claim. He did in fact send Giuliano della Rovere to beg King René's aid. Louis XI was now dead (in 1483), and his daughter Anne of Beaujeu was regent of France. She seemed likely to follow Louis's rather cautious policies but there were a number of aggressive natures at the French Court which she could not control. The young René's claims in Provence and Naples had now, by the death of the Count of Maine and under bequest from his father, fallen to the French Crown. Thus the Pope's threat operated better than it had ever done before. There was also the fact that the French regent felt disposed to trade Provence for Naples as the young René's dominion. This could not have been more embarrassing for Lorenzo, especially when a French envoy stopped in Florence on his way to Rome to urge the Angevin claim. Florence could hardly afford to lose French friendship – and its most important export market. Lorenzo temporised by saying that the Pope's support for this claim had been only an 'afterthought'. In this he hardly echoed the feeling of the people, who wanted to have done with Naples. He himself had written a letter to Giovanni Albino in Naples on the subject of the Duke of Calabria's brutality, in the hope that the King would find a way of extricating himself from it.

The death of Louis XI had also opened up trouble for Milan. The young Duke of Orleans was now urging his claim to that state, and Venice was tending to seek Neapolitan help again, this time against a possible French invasion. Here too Lorenzo did some hard diplomatic work. He brought Ferdinand and Isabella of Spain onto the scene again. The famous humanist Pontano represented Naples, Trivulzio Milan and Vespucci Florence (though he spoke only occasionally). A treaty was a result, though whether Ferrante would honour it was another matter. He was to pay a tribute to the Pope: here Vespucci spoke up for Florence and asked that this might be paid through the Medici bank. The Pope was to forgive Orsini for fighting against him, and he was to abandon Aquila. San Severino was dismissed from papal service and found his way back via Ravenna to Venice, his old master. The peace was signed in August 1486.

It did not mean peace for Lorenzo, however. He heard that Giuliano della Rovere was on his way to prepare a new treaty with Venice, on the pretence of performing a vow at nearby Padua. The same morning, he heard that the Genoese were asking the Venetians for a loan of Ruberto San Severino, presumably for an attack on Milan. In fact, a small Genoese force under Gian Luigi Fieschi attacked Sarzanella, the Florentine castle overlooking Sarzana. Lorenzo went to Pisa to be on hand for an operation that promised to win back all he had lost in his war with Sixtus. He loved the present Pope no more than he had his predecessor ('I can believe any evil of Innocent'), but he knew that he was less competent and that Italy's political state at this moment was fluid enough for him to snatch a few plums without being noticed. On his side were the lords of

Faenza, Mirandola, Bologna and Piombino. Milanese cavalry came down from Parma and a small Neapolitan army landed close to Pisa. On 21 August Sarzana capitulated, and there was hardly a Genoese left at the end of the day. Probably at Lorenzo's intervention, since he had political objectives in the area, the townsfolk were spared.

But no plums fell. The Doge of Genoa, Cardinal Paolo Fregosi, afraid of what his rivals the Adorni might achieve in their present negotiations with the French, handed Genoa's sovereignty over to Ludovico *il Moro* and the Milanese. Lorenzo got back Sarzana but only because it was now useless: Milan commanded the coast north of it. However, it was better than nothing, and at least he could say that his state was well cushioned by satellites such as Faenza. But the fact was that the other states of Italy, and certainly the states north of the Alps, were now getting too strong for Florence. Partly this was true of every Italian state at the time: each was strong only in so far as it could call down the vengeance of the Turks or the French or imperial troops. Italy was beginning to pay heavily for having a pope. Increasingly Italy became a battlefield for foreign powers, and Florence was the first loser thereby.

Lorenzo felt 'old and gouty', though he was not yet thirty-eight. There was not enough money to finance big political schemes, and should he die early, his son Piero was not the kind to achieve neutrality with diplomatic skill. Lorenzo had long ago understood that Italy was

A lunette from the Palazzo Vecchio by Vasari commemorating the war under Lorenzo between the Florentines and the Genoese.

A bust of Lorenzo's eldest
son Piero (1471–1503) by
Verrochio. Piero's succession
to the 'throne' after his father's
death in 1494 was not a success.
Unlike previous Medici he
expected to be treated like a
prince, and finally he had to
flee the city. He was drowned
in the river Garigliano near
Naples during the flight of the
French army from the Spanish
in 1503.

controlled, if it was controlled anywhere, at Rome, and that if Florence
was to continue to count for anything, the Medici family must begin to
influence the College of Cardinals as it had the Signoria. This was why
he worked hard to get his son Giovanni a cardinal's hat. Gradually that
end was being achieved. The King of France had already, in 1483, given
Giovanni an abbey (Font Doulce).

During 1487 Lorenzo negotiated a marriage between his second
daughter, Maddalena, and the Pope's son Franceschetto Cybò which was
a further step in the same policy. Francesco himself was a genial man-
about-town who would do little but help consume the Medici patrimony. At least he did not gamble or keep bad company like Piero – or so
Lorenzo thought, mistakenly. But whatever weaknesses he had, he
would bring the papal account back to the Medici branch in Rome and
presumably keep it there, especially if a Medici in the meantime became
a cardinal. And then this marriage was popular in Florence. It was less so

in Naples, where Lorenzo stood to lose an ally. He wrote to Ferrante that it had all been the Pope's idea, and how could he refuse the poor fellow really? And also King Ferrante must realise that for twelve or thirteen years he had been at loggerheads with the Curia, and inside Florence the blame for that had fallen on himself.

The price for the bastard husband was 4,000 florins (about £172,000), a great deal of money which Lorenzo at the moment could not lay his hands on. There happened to be another of those periodic and unpredictable recessions which was hitting the Medici offices in Bruges and Lyons hard. This may have been why Lorenzo kept writing to the Pope to postpone the wedding, and spare him and Clarice more time with their Maddalena, especially as she was the apple of her mother's eye. There was another, terrible reason for the delay – Clarice's health. She died before she was forty, in July 1487. Her end was sudden, and Lorenzo was absent from Careggi. He had gone to the sulphur baths at Filetta near Siena for his gout. Clarice had given him ten children, seven of whom had lived.

This same year, his son Piero married Alfonsina Orsini, who came to be as heartily disliked in Florence as he was. It was becoming clear that family hopes must be centred on Giovanni, who was steady, astute and close to his father in ideas. He got his cardinal's hat at the age of thirteen, in March 1489. Besides getting the abbey of Font Doulce from the French king when he was seven, he had received from the Pope the richest abbey in Tuscany, that of Passignano, and from Ludovico *il Moro* that of Miramondo. King Ferrante had given him Monte Cassino. Lorenzo had poured pleading envoys on the Pope for years now to achieve this end.

Innocent VIII insisted that the cardinalate be kept secret for three years, until the boy was sixteen, on pain of excommunication. The secret was well kept except that everyone knew about it. There was public rejoicing in Florence. The cardinalate was not yet confirmed. When Innocent died suddenly, a year later, of an apoplectic fit, Lorenzo was terrified. But confirmation came two years after that, on 9 March 1492, and the ceremony was held at the abbey in Fiesole. The Cardinal, now sixteen, rode down into Florence in pomp, through the San Gallo gate to the cathedral. It was the greatest celebration of Lorenzo's life. Nothing was spared. Florence spent the huge sum of 200,000 florins (nearly £9 million today). Every building hung out tapestries and carpets and flags. There were hundreds of torches flickering from roofs and balconies all through the night. Musicians roamed the town in the dead hours. On the following day Mass was celebrated in the cathedral, which was so crowded that the procession could hardly leave the doors. Then there was a banquet at the house in Via Larga. On the occasion of Lorenzo's marriage, his father Piero had been strong enough to make only a quick appearance. The same was now true of Lorenzo. He could neither attend Mass nor eat with his guests. He was, again like his father, carried in on a litter for a moment. That was the last time he saw his favourite son. The Signoria gave Giovanni a fabulous gift of plate. Such an intimate connection with Rome made the city feel safe at last.

Lorenzo wrote Giovanni a long letter of advice on how he was to bear himself in Rome, 'that sink of all iniquity' as he called it. He warned him against those who would try to corrupt him, through envy of his high position at so early an age, and made it clear that the morals of his fellow cardinals might not be as high as he expected. He agreed that 'several' of them were good men, and Giovanni should follow their example and not the others. He pointed out what a different world Christendom would be if the cardinals were all they should be, because in that case the pope would always be a good one too. Giovanni must therefore behave as an ideal cardinal would, and by inference an ideal pope. 'On this first visit to Rome it would be more advisable to listen to others than to speak much yourself.' Also, it would not be difficult for him to bring advantages to his own family and to Florence. He must be the link between the city and the Church (it was clear that Lorenzo foresaw what an important role Giovanni would one day play in Florence once he had become pope). He went on that Giovanni was the youngest cardinal there had ever been. On public occasions he should dress rather less well than the others. He must avoid 'silk and jewels'. Giovanni would show his taste better by collecting ancient things, manuscripts or statuary, and by keeping learned company. He should invite others more often than he was invited. His food should be plain, and above all he should take enough exercise, as cardinals tended to contract sedentary diseases. He should confide in others 'too little rather than too much'. He should get up early in the morning. As he had so many offices to perform, he would find this habit most useful. Also, he should decide in the evening what his programme for the following day was going to be. He would naturally be asking the Pope for favours from time to time but he should not weary him with solicitations. And he should sometimes talk to the Pope about pleasant things which did not touch on office or preferment.

Lorenzo's friends tried to spare him hard work and worry. Once Poliziano, not wishing to alarm him, wrote to his secretary Michelozzi about one of the family who had fallen sick. Lorenzo replied that this had caused him more alarm than the news itself, and that even if he was no longer strong enough to bear sad news firmly, he had had much experience of sad news, what with the death of his father when he was only twenty-one. Experience supplied, he said, what character no longer could.

The last few years had gone quite well politically. His free trade policy had paid off. By a treaty of 1491, England agreed to supply wool to all Italy (except Venice) via Pisa, in return for considerable commercial privileges. Five *consoli del mare* or 'naval consuls' had been elected by the Seventy to deal with all matters concerning the port of Pisa, and the fortification of Livorno and Sarzana against Milanese Genoa.

Lorenzo began to watch the Seventy with a certain amount of suspicion too. As they sat for life, they might easily get out of hand. In 1490 he deprived them of their right to elect the Signoria and gave it back to the *accopiatori*. A *Balìa* of seventeen received full powers to introduce reforms in the electoral system, taxation and the state debt. It is possible that at this time Lorenzo had it in mind to abandon the principle laid down by his great-grandfather Giovanni that a Medici should go to the palace only when called for. He was clearly the centre of power. At the age of forty-five he would qualify to become chief justice himself, which would at least do away with the anxiety of its being in the hands of a potential rival. This was not a desire for personal aggrandisement. For one thing, he was tired, and nothing would have pleased him better than retirement. It was more in the interests of the party that he should become something like the Doge of Venice, elected and hemmed in with a thousand restraints but nevertheless the ruler; a figurehead but nevertheless a guarantee of strong centralised government. The Florentine constitution badly needed something like a presidential system in which the president sat for life. Like Venice, the city could not bear the idea of being governed by kings and dynasties. But unlike Venice, it basically disliked government of any kind: and this was its undoing. By the time it came to be ruled by a Medici dynasty, in the following century, it was already a pawn in the hands of foreigners. It was this that Lorenzo was trying to avoid. The fear was that with his death the party would capsize. The fear was justified. Had there been something like a dogeship ready for Piero, things might have gone better. As it was, the entire system of government collapsed with Piero's flight from Florence. Savonarola is said to have wanted something like a life-dogeship for himself, but he had not the experience or the Medici astuteness. A dogeship would have been popular in Florence had Lorenzo pushed it through, though the big families would have put up a struggle. As it was, he was a dying man.

The *Balìa* of seventeen called in the old black *quattrini* (coins of copper, worth four *denari*) and replaced them with white ones containing two ounces of silver to each pound of copper. The latter were worth one-fifth more than the old *quattrini*. That was no shocking event in itself. But when the government insisted on being paid in the new money while continuing to pay out in the old, there was an outcry. It was plain crooked dealing. No act of Lorenzo's life was so unpopular.

The Medici were by now not simply a ruling family, or even a party. They were a kind of state exchequer. Their solvency was the state's. No one could say where private Medici fortunes began and state funds ended. Lorenzo certainly appropriated public funds at times for his own use, particularly during the 1478 troubles. For a long time this was disbelieved – until the discovery of a document in the Strozzi papers. The Pazzi conspiracy had arisen at the time it did because the Pazzi, being bankers second only to the Medici, knew precisely how badly the Medici banks were doing. After the failure of the conspiracy, and the failure of the Pope's war, it was Renato de' Pazzi's advice, that the Medici must be attacked financially if they were to be brought down, which won the day. This was why Sixtus IV did everything he could to hinder Medici interests in Rome, and Ferrante the same in Naples, at least for a time. The Pope repudiated the Apostolic Chamber's debt to the Medici, and banished Giovanni Tornabuoni from the city. To meet the crisis, Lorenzo had borrowed great sums from minor cousins, whom he eventually repaid by transferring the Cafaggiolo villa and other land in the Mugello to them, though they regarded this as poor compensation. In January 1495, three years after Lorenzo's death, the town of Florence claimed 74,948 florins (the sum mentioned in the Strozzi document) from the Medici trustees as having been paid to Lorenzo in various instalments out of the public funds. It is likely that this sum averted disaster at the time of the Pazzi conspiracy.

Lorenzo's general manager, Francesco Sassetti, was nothing like as efficient as Cosimo's Giovanni Benci. Giovanni Tornabuoni, the chief

Francesco Sassetti at the age of forty-four, a work by Antonio Rossellino's workshop, 1464. Sassetti was Lorenzo's general manager, and less efficient than his predecessor Giovanni Benci under Cosimo. The Medici company almost went bankrupt two years before Lorenzo's death and was in continual difficulty throughout his 'reign'.

influence on the Medici company, was always fighting for his Rome bank at the expense of others, and embroiling himself with Bruges or Lyons or some other foreign branch. The branches were a mass of inner jealousies. During the last two years of Lorenzo's life, the Medici company came very near to bankruptcy, and Lorenzo seemed to lack the capital to be able to do anything about it. It was a general trend. Between 1422 and 1470, the number of banks operating in Florence had slowly dwindled from seventy-two to thirty-three. Two years after Lorenzo's death, they could be counted on the fingers of one hand. Lorenzo's son Piero was a spender, but so was his brother, the Cardinal, intelligent though he was. Usually such natures are symptomatic of declining business rather than accidents. Had the Medici régime not collapsed, due to Piero's impulsive tactics, the Medici company would almost certainly have run into spectacular trouble. On the other hand, had the bank been at the top of its form, as under Cosimo, Piero's impulsiveness and arrogance would no more have threatened his position than the same faults in half the princes of Italy threatened theirs.

Lorenzo, while lacking the resources, still had the expensive commitments of a great prince. He continued to pay out vast sums for the reception of foreigners and for his secret service. Many lords in the papal possessions were in his pay. Gifts had to be sent abroad constantly to keep powerful princes friendly. France's regent, Anne of Beaujeu, was insatiable in this respect, and the Lyons branch paid out a fortune in *beveraggi* or tips to her. Yet all this was done with surprisingly low taxation in Florence. In the last four years of Lorenzo's life, direct taxation yielded only 225 florins more than it had in 1471 when he started his 'reign'. The crisis which started from the Lyons branch in 1484 was due partly to the extravagance of its managers, who lived like princes. By 1489 the state seemed deceptively prosperous again. Taxation was even on the decrease. In the last two years of Lorenzo's reign, the building trade was doing better than ever before in Florence.

These days, his *coups* were mostly diplomatic. He succeeded in his trade negotiations with Egypt. In 1487 that country had sent its embassy to Florence with the right to confer full trading privileges on the city. The Soldan of Egypt sent with them fabulous gifts for Lorenzo and the Signoria, including balsam, musk, civet, fine muslin, striped tents and a number of animals, among them long-tailed sheep and a giraffe. As Florence had never seen a giraffe before, it was led in great pomp round the city and shown to all the convents. The sheep went to Lorenzo's farms. The giraffe was given a stable in the Via della Scala. It disliked the cold, and great fires were kept alight round its stall night and day in the winter. Florence was in love with it. Its death in January 1489 caused great sorrow. The insatiable Anne of Beaujeu asked Lorenzo to send it to her. She talked about nothing else to the Florentine envoys, and remembered it for years afterwards.

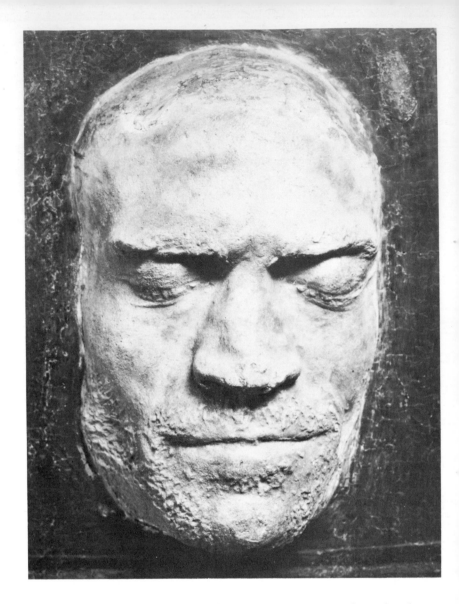

The death mask of Lorenzo the Magnificent. It was Verrocchio who made the death-mask a fashion in Florence, and this one of Lorenzo, who died in 1492, was his work.

Lorenzo's worst enemy, Girolamo Riario, was caught at last by an assassin's knife. This may or may not have been organised – or at least subsidised – by Lorenzo, but it was a great relief when it happened. Riario was at that time ruling Forli, much hated for his heavy taxes and – when he remitted the taxes on the peasantry – for his failure to keep up a royal Court and a decently fed and clothed army. The murder was arranged between two of his courtiers, Lorenzo and Cecco Orsi, together with two mercenary captains. He went to his apartment after dinner one evening and happened to be leaning out of the window, gazing down at the *piazza*, cushions under his elbows. The courtiers entered the room and greeted him. He turned round cheerfully, and Lorenzo Orsi pretended to offer him a petition. Instead, he thrust a knife into him from below – always considered the best method of assassination by those who knew. Girolamo, still alive, ran towards his wife's apartments, but fell. He crawled under the table but the murderers poured blows on him. His body was then flung out of the window. The people dragged it about the streets as Jacopo de' Pazzi's body had been dragged about Florence. The courtiers then arrested Caterina Sforza, Riario's wife, and his children, but the commandant of the castle to which they were taken refused to allow them in without Caterina's approval. She arranged to enter the castle to persuade him, leaving her children with the murderers. The gates were closed behind her. When she refused to leave again, the conspirators threatened to kill her children, but she shouted down to them 'Do what you like! They can be replaced!' As it was, the rebels had to flee from Milanese and Bolognese troops who had entered the town. Caterina Sforza was restored to power, and Lorenzo sent some troops across the Appenines to make sure that no one else like Ludovico *il Moro* stepped in. Later she married Lorenzo's cousin – after her lover (the son of the castle commandant) had been safely murdered.

Florence was now well cushioned with buffer states, thanks to Lorenzo's policy of consolidation. He arranged a marriage between Galeotto Manfredi, lord of Faenza, and Francesca Bentivoglio of Bologna. It was a sad marriage, to say the least. He was unfaithful, and she was jealous. Her assassins got him as he was getting into bed one night: she rose from her pillows and gave him the thrust that killed him. Her father, Giovanni, came down with an army and occupied the town. Then the armed peasants of Val Lamone, Florentine territory, marched on Faenza and sent him packing. They were backed by Lorenzo's troops, who took him prisoner. The Florentine candidate for Faenza's throne, a member of the Astorre family, was then quietly installed. Lorenzo released Giovanni Bentivoglio after giving him a talking-to – and for months afterwards his villa at Poggio a Caiana was not considered safe from a Bolognese raid. But Faenza was in his pocket.

South of Florence, Perugia fell into the hands of the Baglioni family. They banished the Oddi family with Lorenzo's approval, and acknowledged the rule of the Pope while following the orders of the Medici. Niccolò Vitelli of Città di Castello, another papal dependency, was in Lorenzo's pay too. Lorenzo also had a close financial alliance with the Orsini of Bracciano, which meant that he had his hand close to the Pope's neck in case of trouble. Nearly all of central Italy was tied to him by strings of some sort.

He had one enemy left, the Duke of Calabria. The King of Naples, under his influence, had disregarded the treaty which he had just made with the Pope, and had exterminated the rebel barons. The Duke had murdered the Pope's governor and his garrison in Aquila. For five years, Lorenzo patiently mediated between the two sides, and that there was no war in the last years of his life was due entirely to his diplomatic genius. Sometimes it was too much for his nerves and he would fly into a rage. He was heard to say one day that he wished that the King of France governed Italy. He bitterly wanted to retire and spend the rest of his life at Careggi. But he knew that a war was more dangerous to commercial Florence than to any other city in the peninsula. He was much concerned about relations between France and Germany too, in case they fought a war on Italian soil. That was why he kept up close relations with Emperor Maximilian as well as Charles VIII of France. It was an expensive business, being friendly with great princes, but the alternative was too terrible to think about.

A painting by Francesco Granacci (1469–1543) showing the entry of French troops into Florence under their King Charles VIII, two years after Lorenzo's death. Piero, Lorenzo's son, surrendered Pisa, Pietrasanta and Livorno to Charles without a fight. After this he was barred entry to Florence's Signoria.

At the beginning of 1492, war between Charles and Maximilian seemed virtually certain. They both threatened to interfere in Milan after Ludovico *il Moro*'s marriage to the clever and handsome Beatrice d'Este, who made it clear that she was Milan's duchess and not the official one. One faction (Ludovico's) was supported by Charles, the other (the young Duke of Milan's) by Maximilian. Until now, Lorenzo's agent at Lyons, Sassetti, had assured him in his letters that war was out of the question, due to French lack of finances. In a new despatch, he warned Lorenzo that this was no longer the case.

Lorenzo never opened the letter. He was taken to the Careggi villa in

March 1482. He lay in one of the rooms overlooking the estate to the south, in the direction of Florence. Agnolo Poliziano and Lorenzo's sister Bianca were at his side most of the time. His doctors broke the news to Bianca that there was no hope. A priest was called to deliver the last sacraments. Lorenzo would not take them in bed, and had himself carried to the next room, where he managed to sit up. He told his sister that he would not have 'my Lord and God' come to him, but he to Him.

He did not die at once, and some doubts started as to whether his doctors were right. Ludovico *il Moro* sent his doctor, Pier Perleone of Spoleto, who prepared an elixir of pulverised pearls and jewels which was ineffectual. Lorenzo called his son Piero to his bedside and begged him to hold the public welfare higher than his own, which was like asking Piero for the moon. He also urged him to be like a father to his younger brother Giovanni. He entrusted his brother Giuliano's child to Giovanni. One day, he asked desperately for Pico della Mirandola, who came at once from Florence. Lorenzo excused himself for having given him the trouble of coming, but he would die more happily for having seen him again. Then he and Pico and Poliziano talked together in the old way, and the death of the flesh seemed to lose its importance.

The bell of the San Marco monastery where Girolamo Savonarola was abbot. It rang to announce his sermons. He castigated the rich but was tolerated by Lorenzo de' Medici, who, like most of his closest friends, was deeply influenced by Savonarola's preaching. The Dominican warned that only a false happiness could be derived from wealth.

Lorenzo was also visited by Savonarola, and much legend attaches to this visit. Agnolo Poliziano witnessed the interview, and wrote a short memoir about it – but two months after the event. The other man who wrote about it was not there: he simply heard about it from Savonarola. First, there is disagreement about whether Savonarola went of his own volition (doubtful in such a proud man) or whether Lorenzo called for him. The truth may well be that Lorenzo did the calling because he was still Florence's ruler and party-chief: Savonarola's power over the people could not be disregarded, and a last meeting had its political uses. Also, such being the nature of Savonarola's hold on people's minds, the family may have felt that a word from him might secure a passage to heaven, even recovery. After all, Pico della Mirandola, one of Savonarola's most passionate followers, was with Lorenzo. Pico left the room as Savonarola came in, and it is not difficult to imagine that he persuaded Lorenzo to receive him, or acted as go-between. According to Poliziano's letter on the interview to a friend, written in Latin and intended for publication, this is roughly how the conversation went:

SAVONAROLA *(immediately on entering the room)*: I urge you to keep the faith.
LORENZO: I hold it unshaken.
SAVONAROLA: You must swear to lead the purest life from now on.
LORENZO: I shall earnestly strive to do that. If death must come I shall bear it with courage.
SAVONAROLA: Nothing is pleasanter than death if God so wills it. *(Savonarola turns to go but Lorenzo calls him back.)*
LORENZO *(calling after him)*: Oh, father, your blessing before you go!

Savonarola returned and began praying for him, while Lorenzo sat up against his pillows, his head down, answering the prayer word for word from memory. The family was crying, but Lorenzo showed no grief whatsoever.

According to the other witness, Fra' Silvestro, Savonarola's amanuensis, Lorenzo lay dying in agonies of remorse. We already recognise the hysterical tone of so many accounts written by simple men in monasteries. Lorenzo, the story goes, had received many blessings from priests, but he knew that these, being bought with Medici money, were useless to bring him to heaven. 'I know of only one honest friar', he said, and sent for Savonarola.

LORENZO *(as Savonarola enters)*: Three sins lie heavily on my conscience – my sack of Volterra, my curtailment of state dowries to needy brides, and my bloody vengeance on the Pazzi conspirators.
SAVONAROLA *(touched by Lorenzo's desperate state)*: God is good and merciful. But three things are necessary.
LORENZO: What are they, father?
SAVONAROLA *(his face growing stern)*: First a living faith in God's mercy.
LORENZO: In that I have the fullest faith.

An anonymous fifteenth-century oil painting showing the burning of Girolamo Savonarola in the Piazza Signoria, Florence, in 1498. After the flight of Lorenzo's son Piero from Florence Savonarola governed the state for three years of increasing puritanism and confusion. He was burned at the stake after he had recklessly incurred the anger of Roderigo Borgia, Pope Alexander VI.

SAVONAROLA: Then you must restore the ill-gotten wealth you have extorted, or ask your son to do it in your name.

LORENZO (*nodding with effort*): !

SAVONAROLA (*rising and seeming to soar above his real height, while Lorenzo cowers before him*): Lastly you must restore liberty to Florence.

At this Lorenzo summoned all his strength to turn his back on Savonarola angrily (a difficult thing to do in bed, especially when one is dying). Savonarola (merciful as always) promptly left the room, presumably sending to the Devil one of the most humane and studiously just men who have ever lived. Fra' Silvestro's story ends with Lorenzo dying shortly afterwards, tortured by remorse.

As to Savonarola's three demands, they are unlikely since they do not

make sense. Savonarola was not so devoid of political experience as to ask for what could not be realised or even properly understood: to whom Medici wealth was to be restored, to whom liberty was to be given in a moment and how, not even Fra' Silvestro would have been able to say. But it is possible that there was a brisk exchange between the two men, and that Lorenzo found Savonarola's criticisms too wide of the facts to be serious. Yet Lorenzo was troubled by the appalling contradictions into which power led any prince. He once said that a genuine artist must be a gentleman by nature, and it was perhaps the sadness of his life that the same could not be said of the ruler, much less of the party-chief. It was desirable to be a gentleman, but one had to ride with the rascals sometimes:

Quanto sia vana ogni speranza nostra,
quanto fallace ciaschedun disegno,

quanto sia il mondo d'ignoranzia pregno
la maestra del tutto, Morte, il mostra.

Altri si vive in canti e in balli e in giostra,
altri a cosa gentil muove lo ingegno,
altri il mondo ha, e le sue cose, a sdegno,
altri quel che drenti ha, fuor non dimostra.

Vane cure e pensier, diverse sorte
per la diversita che da Natura,
si vede ciascun tempo al mondo errante.

Ogni cosa è fugace e poco dura,
tanto Fortuna al mondo è mal constante;
solo sta ferma e sempre dura Morte.

How vain all our hopes are, how fallacious every design, how full the world is of ignorance: this is shown by the mistress of everything, Death. Some live in song and dance and joust, some are moved in their spirits by gentle things, some hold the world and its objects in disdain, some do not show outside what they have inside. All the time in this erring world we notice hopeless cares and thoughts, and different kinds of fate, according to Nature's diversity. Everything is fleeting, and lasts little, and fortune in this world is never constant. Only Death remains firm and always hard.

There was tremendous grief at Lorenzo's death (on 8 April 1492), especially among the people. His body was removed to San Marco, then carried by priests to San Lorenzo and the family burial place in the old sacristy. The funeral was scrupulously simple. No monuments were erected. As always when a great man died, people noticed terrible portents. Two days before the end came, lightning had struck the cathedral's cupola and put the lantern out. Great marble blocks fell through the roof. Lorenzo, it was said, had realised that he must die when he heard that the lightning had struck on the Careggi side of the cupola. The lions that were by tradition caged close to the cathedral as symbols of the city fought each other for the first time. And so on.

The Spoletan doctor who had failed to cure Lorenzo threw himself down a well. Some say that he was killed by members of Lorenzo's household but he probably went mad, committing suicide after being taken to the nearby Martelli villa. The Signoria, the Colleges and the four Councils voted an address of condolence to Lorenzo's sons which was carried by 483 votes to sixty-three. The size of the 'nays' points to the strong anti-Medici feeling: this had always been there but now it was bold enough to come forward.

On 12 April 1492, Giovanni wrote to his brother Piero from Rome, 'What a father we have lost! How sympathetic he was with his children!' He went on to say that he would obey Piero as a father in everything: and

OPPOSITE Interior wall of the Medici chapel. Opposite the tribute by Michelangelo to Guiliano, Lorenzo's son, is a complimentary monument to his grandson, Lorenzo. At the feet of the Duke recline the figures of twilight and dawn, lamenting the death of the princes.

then a warning, which reads like a portent, 'Allow me, however, my own Piero, to express my hope that in your behaviour towards people, especially those round you, I may find you as I would wish – kindly, liberal, friendly, humane.'

It was not long before Italy realised that it had lost its chief statesman. Naples, Milan, Venice, Rome were suddenly at each other's throats. Each of them realised that for the past ten years hardly one important decision of foreign policy had been reached without Lorenzo's being informed beforehand and consulted for his opinion. He had kept the Italian peace single-handed. Only now was his role fully realised. King Ferrante said when he heard of Lorenzo's death, 'This man lived long enough to be most worthy of his own immortality, but not long enough for Italy.' Every prince in Europe wrote a letter of condolence to the house in Via Larga.

Innocent VIII died not long after Lorenzo. His successor was the terrible Roderigo Borgia (Alexander VI). Piero de' Medici soon showed that he was incapable of imitating his father, as he tried for a time to do. It was not that he lacked intelligence or learning, even a certain goodness. But he expected to be treated like a prince. He quickly made a treaty with the Pope and Naples, at a time at which he should have been trying to keep Ludovico il Moro away from Charles VIII of France. Instead, Ludovico was his enemy in a matter of days. French troops were soon in Italy. The Italian princes now realised, all too late, what the meaning of Lorenzo's work had been. They saw that their independence was at an end, for the simple reason that they had failed to see how weak they each were, compared with the new nations north of the Alps. Ludovico il Moro bitterly regretted what he had done. He wrote to Piero in the hope that he would find a way of calling the French off from their objective of conquering Naples. Piero interviewed Ludovico's envoy, having posted Charles VIII's man behind a door to listen. He wanted to prove that Ludovico was no ally for the French to have. It was a disastrous way of conducting diplomacy, and could be calculated to leave Florence without a friend in the world; which is what happened.

When Ludovico and Charles VIII each heard of this incident, Piero lost all the credit his father had built up in a lifetime. The French attacked Sarzana, pillaging and raping, and looked as though they meant to come to Florence. Piero thought that he would repeat his father's boldness when, in a similarly hopeless situation, he had thrown himself on an enemy's mercy. He went to Charles VIII's camp, but was treated like a servant. He then offered to give up not only Sarzana but Pietrasanta, Pisa and Livorno. On his return to Florence, he was barred entrance to the Signoria. He fled to Venice. French troops entered Florence unresisted. The Medici house was plundered. In a day, the precious library, the collection of vases and statuary and cameos was largely destroyed.

Lorenzo's 'Court' had dispersed. Agnolo Poliziano and Pico della

Mirandola died not long afterwards. Poliziano was forty and Pico della Mirandola, worn out by his studies, thirty-two. It now looked as if Florence was happy to be rid of the Medici 'tyranny', as it had now become. The city was divided between the *Frateschi* or followers of Savonarola and the *Compagnacci* or conservative party of big families. Alexander VI, the new Pope, was behind the *Compagnacci*. Children fought in the streets on the issues between them. In 1497 Piero tried a come-back with the help of Venetian troops and the Orsini family, but he bungled even this. His chief supporters inside the city were beheaded, the rest were banished or imprisoned. The Savonarola party later insisted that all of them be put to death. Among them was Lorenzo Tornabuoni.

There was a ridiculous 'trial by fire' between Savonarola and one of his opponents, a Franciscan and protégé of the *Compagnacci*. Faggots were lit in the Piazza della Signoria but the two sides argued until the flames had died. A kind of madness had taken hold of Florence, and Savonarola's rule seemed an expression of it. After three years of government by sermon, Savonarola was burned by force. Piero too perished. He joined the French under their new King, Louis XII, and was drowned in the River Garigliano in an engagement with Spanish troops.

Medici rule was re-established in 1513 when Giovanni returned as Pope Leo X and the city's first prince. He put Florence and the Medici possessions in order again. But he had come under the wing of a Spanish army. The city was never again a major state. In 1530 Giuliano de' Medici's illegitimate son Giuliano, now Pope Clement VII, invited the Emperor Charles V to sack Florence as he had sacked Rome three years before. That was the final eclipse of the Renaissance. Those long discussions with Poliziano and Pico and Marsilio Ficino going far into the night, were difficult to imagine in this new Florence. Lorenzo's memory too went into eclipse.

A medal of Pope Leo X probably cast immediately after his death in 1521. Leo X (Giovanni de' Medici) was the youngest cardinal of his day and his election to the papacy was assiduously planned over the years by his father, who saw Florence's future after his own death as lying in a close understanding with the Vatican. After eighteen years of exile the Medici family returned to Florence in 1512 under Leo X as the city's first prince. From that time the Medici had the official title of Duke, later Grand Duke, and the city was virtually a papal satellite.

Bibliography

C. M. ADY, *Lorenzo de' Medici and Renaissance Italy*, London 1955.

E. ARMSTRONG, *Lorenzo de' Medici and Florence in the Fifteenth Century*, London 1896.

E. BARFUCCI, *Lorenzo de' Medici e la societa artistica del suo tempo*, Florence 1945.

G. BIAGI, *The Private Life of the Renaissance Florentines*, London 1896.

E. BIZZARRI, *Il Magnifico Lorenzo*, Verona 1950.

M. BRION, *Laurent le Magnifique*, Paris 1937.

J. BURCKHARDT, *The Civilization of the Renaissance in Italy*, London 1878.

J. CARTWRIGHT, *The Painters of Florence*, London 1900.

E. CECCHI, *Lorenzo il Magnifico*, Rome 1949.

L. EINSTEIN, *The Italian Renaissance in England*, London 1902.

J. EWART, *Cosimo de' Medici*, London 1899.

W. K. FURGUSON, *The Renaissance in Historical Thought*, Boston (Mass.) 1948.

E. L. S. HORSBROUGH, *Lorenzo the Magnificent*, London 1905.

LORENZO DE' MEDICI, *Opere*, 2 vols, Bari 1913.

G. PIERACCINI, *La stirpe de' Medici di Cafaggiolo*, Florence 1924.

H. PIRENNE, *History of Europe*, London 1955.

N. ROBB, *The Neoplatonism of the Italian Renaissance*, London 1935.

R. DE ROOVER, *The Medici Bank*, Oxford 1948.

R. DE ROOVER, *The Rise and Decline of the Medici Bank*, Cambridge (Mass.) 1963.

W. ROSCOE, *The Life of Lorenzo de' Medici*, London 1895.

J. A. SYMONDS, *Renaissance in Italy*, London 1875–1886

TOURING CLUB ITALIANO, *La Toscana*,

G. F. YOUNG, *The Medici*, London 1910.

List of Illustrations

Index